**ASPATORE
BOOKS**

About Aspatore Books
Business Intelligence From Industry Insiders
www.Aspatore.com

Aspatore Books publishes only the biggest names in the business world, including C-level (CEO, CTO, CFO, COO, CMO, Partner) leaders from over half the world's 500 largest companies and other leading executives. Aspatore Books publishes the Inside the Minds, Bigwig Briefs, ExecEnablers and Aspatore Business Review imprints in addition to other best selling business books and journals. By focusing on publishing only the biggest name executives, Aspatore Books provides readers with proven business intelligence from industry insiders, rather than relying on the knowledge of unknown authors and analysts. Aspatore Books focuses on publishing traditional print books, while our portfolio company, Big Brand Books focuses on developing areas within the book-publishing world. Aspatore Books is committed to providing our readers, authors, bookstores, distributors and customers with the highest quality books, book related services, and publishing execution available anywhere in the world.

The *Inside the Minds* Series
Real World Intelligence From Industry Insiders
www.InsideTheMinds.com

Inside the Minds was conceived in order to give readers actual insights into the leading minds of business executives worldwide. Because so few books or other publications are actually written by executives in industry, *Inside the Minds* presents an unprecedented look at various industries and professions never before available. Each chapter is comparable to a white paper and is a very future oriented look at where their industry/profession is heading. In addition, the *Inside the Minds* web site makes the reading experience interactive by enabling readers to post messages and interact with each other, become a reviewer for upcoming books, read expanded comments on the topics covered and nominate individuals for upcoming books. The *Inside the Minds* series is revolutionizing the business book market by publishing an unparalleled group of executives and providing an unprecedented introspective look into the leading minds of the business world.

About Big Brand Books

Big Brand Books assists leading companies and select individuals with book writing, publisher negotiations, book publishing, book sponsorship, worldwide book promotion and generating a new revenue stream from publishing. Services also include white paper, briefing, research report, bulletin, newsletter and article writing, editing, marketing and distribution. The goal of Big Brand Books is to help our clients capture the attention of prospective customers, retain loyal clients and penetrate new target markets by sharing valuable information in publications and providing the highest quality content for readers worldwide. For more information please visit www.BigBrandBooks.com or email jonp@bigbrandbooks.com.

INSIDE THE MINDS

INSIDE THE MINDS:
Leading
Consultants

*Industry Leaders Share Their Knowledge on
the Art of Consulting*

**ASPATORE
BOOKS**

Published by Aspatore Books, Inc.

For information on bulk orders, sponsorship opportunities or any other questions please email store@aspatore.com. For corrections, company/title updates, comments or any other inquiries please email info@aspatore.com.

First Printing, November 2001
10 9 8 7 6 5 4 3 2 1

ISBN 1-58762-059-6

Library of Congress Card Number: 2001119341

Cover design by Michael Lepera/Ariosto Graphics & Kara Yates

Material in this book is for educational purposes only. This book is sold with the understanding that neither any of the authors or the publisher is engaged in rendering legal, accounting, investment, or any other professional service.

This book is printed on acid free paper.

A special thanks to all the individuals that made this book possible.

Special thanks to: Jo Alice Hughes, Rinad Beidas, Kirsten Catanzano, Melissa Conradi

The views expressed by the individuals in this book do not necessarily reflect the views shared by the companies they are employed by (or the companies mentioned in this book). The companies referenced may not be the same company that the individual works for since the publishing of this book.

ASPATORE BUSINESS REVIEW
Tear Out This Page and Mail or Fax To:

Aspatore Books, PO Box 883, Bedford, MA 01730
Or Fax To (617) 249-1970

Name:

Email:

Shipping Address:

City: State: Zip:

Billing Address:

City: State: Zip:

Phone:

Lock in at the Current Rates Today-Rates Increase Every Year
Please Check the Desired Length Subscription:

1 Year ($1,090) _____   2 Years (Save 10%-$1,962) _____
5 Years (Save 20%-$4,360) _____   10 Years (Save 30%-$7,630) _____
Lifetime Subscription ($24,980) _____

(If mailing in a check you can skip this section but please read fine print below and sign below)
Credit Card Type (Visa & Mastercard & Amex):

Credit Card Number:

Expiration Date:

Signature:

Would you like us to automatically bill your credit card at the end of your
subscription so there is no discontinuity in service? (You can still cancel your
subscription at any point before the renewal date.) Please circle: Yes   No

***(Please note the billing address much match the address on file with your credit
card company exactly)**

Terms & Conditions
We shall send a confirmation receipt to your email address. If ordering from Massachusetts, please
add 5% sales tax on the order (not including shipping and handling). If ordering from outside of the
US, an additional $51.95 per year will be charged for shipping and handling costs. All issues are
paperback and will be shipped as soon as they become available. Sorry, no returns or refunds at any
point unless automatic billing is selected, at which point you may cancel at any time before your
subscription is renewed (no funds shall be returned however for the period currently subscribed to).
Issues that are not already published will be shipped upon publication date. Publication dates are
subject to delay-please allow 1-2 weeks for delivery of first issue. If a new issue is not coming out for
another month, the issue from the previous quarter will be sent for the first issue. For the most up to
date information on publication dates and availability please visit www.Aspatore.com.

Inside the Minds:
Leading Consultants

*Industry Leaders Share Their Knowledge on
the Art of Consulting*

CONTENTS

Frank Roney   **9**
*THE DRIVE FOR BUSINESS RESULTS:
WALKING IN THE CUSTOMER'S SHOES*

Randolph C. Blazer   **27**
UNDERSTANDING THE CLIENT

Pamela McNamara   **57**
*WORKING AT THE INTERFACE
OF TECHNOLOGY AND BUSINESS*

Dr. Chuck Lucier   **95**
*OVERLAP YOUR CIRCLES: MAXIMIZING
THE THREE ELEMENTS OF THE STRATEGY
CONSULTING BUSINESS*

Dietmar Ostermann   **129**
*THE ART OF CONSULTING-FIGURING OUT
HOW TO DO IT RIGHT*

Luther J. Nussbaum   **147**
THE DISCIPLINE OF CLIENT VALUE

Bradley M. Smith   **187**
GIVING CLIENTS MORE THAN THEY EXPECT

Thomas J. Silveri   **207**
TAILORING SOLUTIONS TO MEET CLIENT NEEDS

David Frigstad   **227**
THE FUTURE OF MARKETING CONSULTING

John C. McAuliffe   **251**
THE RULES HAVE CHANGED

THE DRIVE FOR BUSINESS RESULTS: WALKING IN THE CUSTOMER'S SHOES

FRANK RONEY

IBM

General Manager,
Worldwide Business Innovation Services

The Consulting Path

I've been in professional services for 24 years. It's an intoxicating profession. IBM's consultants live at the intersection of business strategy and technology execution, and it's constantly changing in both areas. There's never a boring day, a boring assignment, or a boring engagement. Our customers' business designs are evolving as new applications of technologies emerge.

At the core, the consulting industry is all about creating value for our customers, and ultimately for their customers. But it's also about hard work and staying on the leading edge of change while being practical about what can and cannot be done. Today, creating value has everything to do with the transformation to e-business.

In the early 1990s, as technology became a key enabler for business strategy, we saw a real acceleration of consulting around technology. It was driven by ERP systems and by the opportunity to reengineer businesses, to take out costs and become more productive and efficient. That increased throughout the 1990s, particularly around the Y2K technology changeover.

With the initial emergence of the Internet and the first wave of e-business, we saw an insatiable demand for leading consulting talent – talent that could develop strategies, create new business models, and implement technologies that drive a company's growth, increase their competitive advantage, save money, or all of the above.

Then, in the last two years, we saw a surge around some very big ideas propelled by the business designs of the dot-coms. As we now know, it was short lived. The dot-coms learned the hard lesson that ideas and innovation without tangible business results isn't going to cut it. The best consultants know how to deliver on the promise of big ideas. You have to execute. You have to marry innovation with maximizing shareholder value. The second wave of e-business is all about the hard work of both business innovation and technology integration.

Defining Success

We are maniacally focused on customer value. It's an important element of our mission. In order to know that we're delivering that value, we measure customer satisfaction regularly and then ask ourselves, "Have we helped our customers drive their shareholder value? Have we impacted their revenue growth or increased their market share? Have we impacted their competitiveness? Have we helped to reduce their costs and increase their productivity? Have we contributed to the development of their business strategy or the transformation of their business?"

If you're going to live at the intersection of business strategy and technology execution, as we do, the simple question that must be asked every day is "Have we made a difference to our customers?" If we haven't leveraged technology to further their business strategy and to drive more shareholder value, we haven't done our job. We have another job, too, though. As a publicly owned company and as a publicly owned consultancy, we must also drive value for our own shareholders. Driving value for both our customers and our shareholders is an interesting balance – one that we've been successful at for quite a while now.

Another measure of success, at least for the businesses that we advise, is the ability to unlock and leverage business strategies across an entire enterprise and all of its business processes. It's not about piece-parts. It's about unlocking the promise of e-business throughout a company, in all of its business processes. Consultants must be industry-focused these days. They must be keenly focused on the insights, business designs, new business processes, and technologies that are evolving industry wide. The winning combination is a consultant who can keep the industry at the forefront of his or her mind, and marry that with the right technology to address a customer's business issue – not technology for technology's sake, but technology that has real payoff for customers.

Opportunities

An important opportunity is wireless and mobile computing. It's a key technology for increasing customer loyalty, reducing operational costs, and improving business productivity. We use wireless technology everyday. For businesses, wireless makes it easier to do things like track inventory, improve customer responsiveness, and increase the effectiveness of the sales force. Wireless makes businesses mobile. It allows people to take aspects of their job with them when they're traveling or working directly with their customers. Completely new business models will emerge that take advantage of wireless technologies. Going forward, it's going to have the kind of game-changing effect on companies that Web access did a decade ago. One fascinating potential is that of location-based services that will allow service transportation companies to track the locations of delivery vehicles and make route adjustments based on real-time market demands. Additionally, these location-based services can provide information to emergency services at a local level to immediately locate people in distress who may call in from a cellular phone.

Finally, we think the next big push in e-business is going to be around transforming the workplace. IBM led the world down the path of using the Web to transform core business processes like supply chain, customer relationship management, and e-procurement. What's next are e-

Workplaces. It's doable in the short term, and it can be a big cost saver. We know, because we've done it ourselves within IBM. This first phase has been about efficiency – turning technology, such as enterprise portals, into employee self-service hubs characterized by tools like e-HR, e-meetings, online learning, instant messaging, and corporate yellow pages. Phase Two will be about putting all these piece-parts under one e-Workplace umbrella as an integrated capability to reduce the costs of traditional workplaces and increase the efficiencies of workers.

The Art of Consulting

I think the art of consulting starts with the ability to understand our customers in the context of their business in their industry. I think of every customer's enterprise as a puzzle. Our job is to both listen to the customer and to be very thoughtful. We need to decompose what we hear, assess the parts, and then reassemble them using our insight and our knowledge to help them develop their business strategy. The art is really about both good listening and having a point of view on what to do and how to do it. However, consulting must be about both ideas and execution. Because of the demand for time-to-market, consultants who can get customers into the market with fresh ideas and workable strategies faster than the competition will lead in the marketplace.

The Need for Consultants

Consultants work with clients for many different reasons. Most of our customers are looking for innovation, fresh insight into their business strategies, and ways to leverage technology. They know the hot topics, and they know a number of different directions they could take, but they're looking for specific industry thought leadership and a point of view. Wireless is a great example. They understand wireless, but they come to us to help them think through the right alternatives that will drive business results. In this sense, customers come to a consultant because they are looking for both insight and capability – whether it's for business strategy, managing change, or implementing technologies.

The ideal customer/consultant relationship is when the change agent becomes the trusted business advisor. This requires having the customer's best interests in mind at all times. Sometimes that means saying no to the customer. Sometimes that means changing the direction of critical customer projects. Objectivity is crucial. Consultants operate best when they are held accountable for delivering on their ideas. Increasingly, our customers are saying they want not only the ideas but also the execution. Often our best customer relationships have a healthy dose of creative tension, where ideas are challenged and accountability is held paramount. We think that's about right.

Difficult Aspects of Consulting

From a people perspective, the consulting profession is well known for stretching work-life balance parameters. Operating at the leading edge of business and technology change is challenging. However, in many ways, that's what makes this profession so appealing. I don't think this balance issue is ever going to go away. The breadth of business change in the business world and the new, emerging technologies are putting a lot of demands on consultants today. Unlike ten years ago, when you could more easily master the technology that we had at that time, the current environment requires both adept industry expertise and a much deeper technology competence than ever before. To address this need, we not only go to market by industry, but we've established technology centers of competence. A high premium is put on collaboration and on the sharing and reuse of assets.

Our consultants compete not just on the basis of their industry, technology, or solution capability, but also through their ability to leverage their experience, expertise, and intellectual assets. It is increasingly important to innovate, share, and improve individual productivity and effectiveness by better managing what we "know." Our ability to save, organize, and apply the extensive knowledge within IBM is key to providing distinctive value to our customers. We use knowledge management to provide our professionals with a framework that enables the reuse of insights, best practices, technical frameworks, and solutions. This knowledge sharing and reuse leads to outstanding service that distinguishes IBM Global Services from its competitors.

Roadmaps

Most good consultancies have an underlying methodology. Over the past ten years we have created what we term the "IBM Global Services Method," which is a whole series of structures and methodologies for conducting our consulting business, from strategy engagements to technical implementations. This is also the basis of how we train our people and how we can execute on an end-to-end value proposition. It's an important part of being a world-class consultancy today, but it's not enough. You have to have a deep understanding of industry. Industry roadmaps are very important. We cultivate, develop, and maintain industry roadmaps, which are points of view of where the industry is going, leveraging the combination of thought leadership and business best practices. We also maintain rich technical frameworks in an effort to shorten time-to-market.

We also believe value-nets are an important aspect of how we create customer value. Our preferred strategy is to work with leading independent software vendors and to use their applications as a key enabler for our customers' business needs. Our business partnerships and our value-nets are at the center of creating value for our customers.

Getting up to Speed

The most important thing is to see the industry and the marketplace through the eyes of the customer. It's about looking through the customer's lens at their markets, at their competitors, and at their industry and seeing the environment that they are operating in. We expect our consultants to come to the engagement with that kind of orientation. This broad perspective ensures we can recommend what is best for the customer's enterprise instead of using only standard industry approaches.

We also work hard in the start-up phase of each engagement to understand our customer's technology preferences and their infrastructure. As we go through the project, we use these insights as grounding points for our work. Doing all of this gives us the ability to truly walk in the customer's shoes.

Metrics to Measure Engagements

A consultant will succeed only if customers value their services and are extremely satisfied with the results of their work. Strong client relationships and the delivery of quantifiable business value will lead to consistently satisfied and loyal customers, excellent reference accounts, and repeat business. Consultants must clearly understand and anticipate customer expectations to proactively innovate new solutions to meet their needs. It is imperative that we understand our customer's perception of the value of our services and their satisfaction with the business impact of our services. A consultant's value must be expressed in customer terms with relevant proof points around industry expertise to have credibility in the marketplace. We must support all recommendations with facts.

In addition, I think every consultant needs to talk with their customer everyday. They must have an active dialogue and actively listen. That means being very open to what's working and what's not, and learning the culture and style of our customers. There are many ways to assess the relationship or engagement, whether it's on track or not, but there's nothing better than listening to the customer.

Good Qualities in Consultants

I think the hallmark of a good consultant is becoming a trusted business advisor for the customer. It's important for the customer to have a sense of trust, to be comfortable with the consultant, and vice versa. Straight talk is essential. Lay things on the line, use meaningful words, separate logic from emotion, and talk about the realities – that's what the customer wants. Worry about how recommendations will be implemented. Recommend ways to resolve potential issues within the customer's environment, paying attention to the culture of the customer's enterprise and its impact on the execution of recommendations. Provide a roadmap to success. Listen to the customer to identify issues that may go beyond the question asked, and provide the answers that bring real business value.

Another thing I look for in our consultants is the willingness to say no when it's in the best interest of the client. There are times when we may not know the right answer, or it may take more time to develop the right answer. Sometimes we may disagree with the client on direction. That's okay. What's not okay is refraining from putting honest thoughts on the table or, for whatever reason, failing to work through the necessary logic of an engagement.

I also think that with the complexities in today's world, you have to be a team player, and you have to have the technology at hand to communicate globally. There are a number of enablers for this kind of collaboration and communication. We use Lotus Notes extensively. Consultants need to be able to reach out to their network of colleagues at a moment's notice. Teaming and collaboration skills are extremely important today. At the same time, consultants also need a healthy degree of objectivity. They need to be self-starters who are maniacally focused on delivering customer value. A good consultant thinks about how he or she can add value that goes beyond just following a good work plan.

Pitfalls to Avoid

One of the biggest pitfalls is promising more than you can deliver. We talked about the importance of getting up to speed. The formulation and execution of a customer engagement is not only based on the customer's needs, but also based on understanding the customer's capabilities and resources to support the engagement. The idea of doing what the customer wants, in the time frame they want, with whatever resources they have, may not always be the right plan. It may be over-promising.

Another pitfall is recommending last year's idea or best practice. The market is continuing to evolve at a very fast pace. Consultants must stay current. While we use structures and methods as a core part of how we consult, we also must be highly flexible and innovative. It is important to remember that there is a really creative part to this business. That we had a certain point of view a year ago doesn't mean that point of view won't change as we increase our learning and adjust our insights to keep pace with market dynamics. I also ask our consultants to serve the customer and not just the project. They need to keep that foremost in their minds. Every day they have to think about the customer, their needs, and how the project is serving the customer. We have work plans; we have objectives; and we have deadlines; but at the end of the day, it all comes back to creating customer business value. They must keep the customer's interest foremost in their minds.

Leadership

We've developed a number of competency profiles for our key leaders. Many types of leaders are required to be successful in a large global consultancy. First and foremost, in terms of core competencies, our leaders have to have customer insight. They have to be able to think about business through the customer's eyes. They also have to have the drive and passion to be successful in this business. They have to be able to deliver straight talk. They have to be team players with both the customer and with colleagues across IBM because dynamic teaming is an important part of how we deliver customer value. Our consultants need to be decisive. This profession is exciting because it's at the pinnacle of change and because it's at the intersection of business strategy and technology execution. The ability to lead and provide compelling points of view at that intersection is crucial.

In terms of differentiation, some consultants are visionaries. Others have strong subject matter expertise in business strategy, in industry, in business process, and in technology. Still others are business incubators. All must be change agents and must strive to be recognized as such by their clients.

Golden Rules of Consulting

The first golden rule is that the customer comes first. It's at the pinnacle of what we do at IBM. If you wake up every day thinking about putting your customer first, everything else will fall into place. The second thing I would stress is accountability – the willingness to be held accountable and deliver on our commitments. We want to put innovative and fresh ideas on the table for our customers, but they have to be ideas that are executable. The third golden rule is that everything we do should be about driving customer business results. We can exceed customer expectations only if we deliver real business value.

There are a lot of clichés in this industry, but I think these three rules are important tenets.

The Future of Consulting

The consulting industry is going through massive change. The future is bright for those who can deliver end-to-end value. Today's projects are far more complex than they've ever been, and for that reason customers are looking for globally oriented change agents who can deliver at the intersection of business strategy and technology execution.

It's not easy to be global, or to have insight in each industry and the segments that make up those industries. What we've done here at IBM Global Services is to build the world's leading consultancy and services company from the ground up. It's not something you can go out and acquire and quickly assemble. It takes a strong culture to maintain objectivity and a critical eye for continually improving our execution in the market to make this work. These are different times in our industry. Speed – from strategy design to execution – is key. Ideas will always be important, but those who can crack the code to bridge strategy and technology are going to be the leaders of this industry going forward. Those who can implement their ideas will win.

We're ten years into our journey of building IBM Global Services and IBM's consulting capability. We went from being a very small player to a world leader through a lot of hard work and clear determination. Today we have over 150,000 professionals. We got to where we are by maintaining a strong commitment to putting the customer first, every day. We let them do most of the talking. We listen, provide our point of view, and then execute. I think only a handful of companies are going to be able to deliver the kind of value that global customers need.

Frank Roney is general manager, Business Innovation Services, Worldwide, IBM Global Services. His responsibilities include achieving the growth, market share, and profit targets for BIS globally; developing the BIS strategy and value propositions; managing the BIS global investment portfolio; and validating, on a global basis, that BIS has the right resources and capabilities to deliver the offerings. Mr. Roney leads the five Global BIS Sector Executives, who are responsible for developing industry services strategies, developing thought leadership, and industry specific solutions.

Previously, Mr. Roney was IBM's senior executive responsible for the worldwide systems integration business. This responsibility included establishing the business models and business processes IBM uses worldwide to perform the systems integration business and leading IBM's global systems integration community to ensure consistent business performance.

Before that, Mr. Roney was general manager, Integration Services, U.S., IBM Global Services. He was responsible for the strategy, growth, profitability, and operations of the United States consulting and systems integration business units of IBM Global Services.

Prior to joining IBM in 1993, Mr. Roney was a partner with Price Waterhouse in their Management Consulting Services division, where he managed their Michigan business unit, SAP business unit, and major engagements in a variety of industries, including the automotive, retail/distribution, and consumer product segments.

UNDERSTANDING THE CLIENT

RANDOLPH C. BLAZER

KPMG Consulting, Inc.

Chairman and Chief Executive Officer

The Enjoyable Aspects of Consulting

Although I'm charged with a variety of business responsibilities as CEO, at the end of the day, what I most enjoy and what gets my creative juices flowing is still providing direct assistance to our clients and helping our professionals solve client challenges. Clients primarily come to KPMG Consulting for two reasons: to solve a business problem or pursue a business opportunity. We provide not just analytics, but also experience and industry knowledge, as well as information systems, to support their business on an ongoing basis. Most challenges that companies face today revolve around harnessing the information they have and using it to their advantage. Being integrally involved in solving these concerns is exciting and dynamic, and it keeps me always thinking forward about the next major business and technology innovations to help our clients tackle them.

Second only to working for our clients is the excitement of working with our colleagues, both inside and outside the business. At KPMG Consulting, we are a group of top-notch professionals. Throughout all levels of the organization, everyone you encounter is experienced, committed, intelligent, and eager to learn. It creates an environment that encourages you to work hard, increase your knowledge, and be truly driven toward success. We've created a culture that emphasizes personal responsibility for our individual growth, while at the same time focusing on each other's success and valuing teamwork and collaboration. So, particularly once you begin to accept more responsibility and move to the management levels that help drive the business, it's a great pleasure and a huge responsibility to bring others into the company and help ensure their success. You have to make sure that they're mentored, developed, motivated, and trained to work with the client and that they are performing well and in the clients' best interests. And our mentoring opportunities are enormous; you typically have very diverse teams. That's what drives the creativity. The need for mentoring can go in all directions. We are mentors to those who report to us, those we report to who may not have all the specifics of the client's particular needs, those who work alongside us, and our clients, who often serve key roles on our joint teams. It's a wonderful position to be in, where you can help others grow within a company – a client's or ours – and see them be successful.

The Art of Consulting

The art of consulting starts with a clear understanding of what the need is – the business problem or challenge the client is facing. You have to be experienced first so that you have a solid foundation, and you also have to know a wide range of client specifics before you can even know where and how to start. You have to understand the client, the environment they sit in, and the competitive marketplace they operate in. You have to understand what their competitors are doing. You have to understand their culture, the state of their machinery or apparatus, and whether they're producing goods, generating information, or providing a service. In the art of consulting, you must truly understand the client and the client's situation. I see it as one part relationship building and one part technical analytics of the client's current situation and needs.

Once you've locked onto the need and the aspects of that requirement, you reach the second phase of this art, which is addressing client needs and delivering results through creative solutions and methodologies. Sometimes it involves an approach that has never been tried before. How do you develop an approach or methodology to deliver the results that the client is looking for, while providing enough specialty expertise to guide both you and the client?

The third aspect of this art is the communication process that evolves when you try to keep both the client's needs and the project methodology in lock-step as the project unfolds. As you go through a project, the need will change and become more defined. Your intended solution may begin to drive on one aspect of that need but forget the other aspects. Unless you have constant dialogue going on between those two things, need and delivery, you're going to get out of synch. It's a real art.

Most of our projects kick off with a formal planning stage, which helps make sure roles are clearly defined, that KPMG Consulting and client team members at all levels have a clear understanding of their responsibilities and who specifically is accountable. It also ensures that background information will be provided to get us up to speed quickly and that formal communication plans are in place. We incorporate a change process and approval structure into all of our involved engagements, as well. This helps manage changes to the scope of projects and lets the client and our professionals fully understand the implications of changes across project areas and to cost and resource demands, as well as project timelines. In turn, it helps us mobilize additional personnel as needed and helps keep the project moving, instead of stalling out. The bottom line: We have to make sure that expectations are set, communications are clear, detailed and ongoing feedback is provided, onsite corrections are made, and that we keep going until we get to the result the client wants. And most important: It has to be a lasting result.

The New Face of Consulting – Challenges

The job of and pressures on a consultant have gotten even harder in recent years. I say that primarily because the world is running at a faster speed. We have a faster pace and probably a greater desire for results than we've ever had in the business world. Whether it's getting information instantaneously via e-mail or restructuring their entire business model in six weeks, people expect immediate solutions to complex issues and are often impatient with the exploratory work that must be done to offer real solutions to complicated business needs. So our professionals really have to hit the ground running with the industry acumen and speed with purpose that give clients confidence that their time isn't being wasted. It serves no purpose for consultants to extend the length of client engagements and rack up fees unnecessarily. Ninety-six percent of our top clients are repeat customers because we deliver results – fast.

In addition to the increased sense of urgency, clients and consultants often share a misconception that technology is the great panacea for business problems. But technology both helps and confuses the issue. Technology is an enabler for you to be an effective consultant and solve problems. We've had good success with automated diagnostic and assessment tools and have derived immeasurable benefit from the knowledge-sharing that our intranet permits, to name a few quick examples. But technology also confuses things because people race for technology to solve fundamental business issues. Technology can't do that. This requires experienced people, thinking through the problems and alternatives.

Another recent change that makes the profession seem a little harder is the whole theory around people – your workforce and what their professional desires and goals in life are and what their emotional attitudes are. We talk a lot about the Generation X and the "Me Too" and the "What's in it for me" types who are not willing to put in the hard work and hours required. But this is not a theory I really subscribe to. People are still pretty good; they are dedicated to doing the right things for their clients and their colleagues. If you treat them openly and honestly, they're going to respond the same way people did 30 years ago. We're all rational people, and we're all trying to be fair-minded. We have ambitions and goals, but I think we have to be clearly attentive to people's needs. The notion of how you deal with workforce issues just seems more complicated today, when really it's all about the same good people who have goals, and making sure those goals are understood. It's important to make sure those goals are in lock-step with the organization, so you get a win-win. I feel pretty good about where we stand and what we've done to respond to our people.

If you put all that together, it's the same thing we did 30 years ago. People would say it's the same thing they did 50 years ago. We do it a little faster now, and we're a little more sophisticated. Our generation of consultants has pushed the bar up, and the next generation will take it to the next step, and that's expected.

Has consulting become more difficult? The answer is yes, but the fundamentals are still the same. It's still about locking onto a client, understanding the business need, trying to find a solution to that need, communicating around that solution, and keeping it in lock-step. It's a solution for a need. It's still about hiring a workforce and motivating a workforce that feels like they're going to get something as a result of delivering something to the client. It's about facing challenges and delivering results.

What a Consultant Can do for a Client

The range of consultant involvement can be pretty broad. Sometimes the clients understand their needs and understand how they need to get them solved, but they don't necessarily have the workforce to get it done. Their workforce is already involved in operations and core business roles, and they don't have a special or contingent workforce that they can throw at new requirements or charge with seizing new opportunities. It's not cost-effective for clients to add to their own workforce to get those things done. So it's not always a situation where we can do something that our customers can't; it's that we have the additional professionals to augment their workforce for specific projects.

I think we have a workforce that is very involved and can repeat some of the things we've done in other environments. That's not to say that the same solution works everywhere, because it does not. Not every client will consider or accept a solution that worked somewhere else, because every client is unique. But I think we have to have the ability to see what has worked and what hasn't worked in other environments. If a consultant has been involved in multiple similar projects – for instance, ERP implementations – that a typical customer might need only once, that professional adds real value. He or she knows where the risks are and where typical issues arise. That allows the analytics to say, "This is what has worked there, but this is how it needs to be tweaked here." So the consultant can use those past successes to eliminate much of the groundwork, reduce the risks, and speed up the project to achieve the desired results. Bringing experience A or experience B to the table – that's the second thing we do.

The third thing we do is come at the issue from a more objective point of view, meaning we're not caught up in the culture or some of the issues clients may face internally. We can foresee solutions more clearly than they can at certain points in time and may be able to punch toward those solutions when their own workforce may be mired in organizational issues, responsibilities, or preferences.

We can bridge those issues for them more easily. But I don't think the impression should ever be that we can do something our clients can't. I think, because of our objectivity from experience and augmentation, we can help the client punch through on something that would not be as time- or cost-effective for them to do themselves.

The New Face of Consulting – Opportunities

One could talk about areas of growth functionally and say the whole sales force automation world is an area ripe for improvement and a great opportunity for consultants. It's clear that companies can gain a lot in terms of the way they service their customers. There's a lot of work and a lot of growth in that area. Within the supply chain, the logistics of manufacturers and distributors, products and services – there's still a lot of work to be gained there. For example, in our own business, I would point to the whole globalization arena. As a business, we focus on the Global 2000 client marketplace. There are very few Global 2000 companies today that do run their financials as one global entity. They have different regions and different product service divisions, which all run their own sets of financials or their reports on customers, supply chain vendors, and resource management. What I think happens is that companies truly need to be global, so they can be real-time, and so they can have virtual closes.

I can tell you at the end of a particular period, within a very short time, where the company stands on our financials. Traditionally companies close their books on the 30th of the month. So by the 15th or 20th day of the next month, they start to know what their financials are for a period that closed two or three weeks earlier. You're already two to three weeks away from making corrections if the numbers don't come out the way you want them. The question is, "How do you get all that pushed so that activity happens, and your financial status and your logistic or engineering status is all real-time or virtual-time, so you can see where you are against your key indicators?" I think there are going to be tremendous opportunities to help clients make progress in that area.

Another area where there will be growth is broadband technologies. Technologies are being developed in our communication firms across the world. How do we utilize them in our businesses? We do interviews on the phone, but we could be webcast, face-to-face, on a broadband line. Would that make for a better interview, a richer interview?

The answer is probably yes. Someday the cost of doing that and the infrastructure that needs to exist to support it will be so commonplace that of course we'll do it that way, and people will interact with that. We're going to get involved in all those areas; they are all areas for growth.

I think it's important for a consultant to be focused on two things: One is the state of technology – the traditional answer if you're a consultant. But it's only half of the challenge and the opportunity.

The other half of the opportunity is staying focused on the client's business needs. Trends come and go, and focusing on hot technologies or slick solutions won't keep clients. You have to stay focused on the client, put yourself in the client's shoes, and understand what the client's needs are. What drives their business? What are the things they worry about the most? What do they have to change and improve upon to become competitive? That drives the business need, which can then pull technology to make it happen. You have to be involved in both of those things. KPMG Consulting, as an integrator, is involved in both of those two aspects, and that goes back to the art of consulting. It makes consulting, consulting. It is not a commodity business. One size does not fit all, but there are some common threads that you can clearly do to make your services efficient.

Focus, focus, focus. Understand every aspect of that need, but don't lose focus and start doing 28 other things that could interfere. Stay locked on the issue at hand and punch through. It's better to punch through on one thing than to try to dabble in 28 things.

And be patient. Good results, results that last a lifetime, don't come overnight. Stick to the methodologies and don't skip steps. Be patient and follow through in every element.

The Real Value of a Consultant - Success

Success for our clients means that they've achieved the ends they've set out to achieve. If they've identified a need, we've helped them to solve it, or helped them seize an opportunity. Another measure of success is that the solutions have staying power. It's not just a one-time fix, but also a fix that can support them in their opportunity area over a period of time.

No matter what happens in terms of our internal execution and the delivery against those needs, the ultimate test of client satisfaction is, "Was the client fulfilled, and did we help them become more successful?" Of course, we'll go back internally to look at the metrics to see if we did the job on time, if we made any money, if we got a challenge out of it, if our people got an opportunity to propel themselves forward, etc. There's a whole host of internal things we examine. But the first test is, "Did the client get something out of it that enabled them to move forward?"

To support that, every time we get involved with a client, a company like ours stands behind our work. We've done it for a hundred years, and we'll keep doing it into the next hundred years. One thing that drives us is, regardless of whether this cost us a little bit more money or not, "Did we get the result we wanted?" That's ultimately the question we ask. Instead of how much more did this cost us, the question becomes, "Was the customer satisfied? Did we help the client move forward as a business?"

We look for ongoing partnerships with our clients. The relationship has to be one in which we are supporting each other in moving forward, so we are both successful. Our job as business advisors and integrators is to support our clients by understanding their need, delivering on that need, and keeping that need and delivery in cost and balance with each other. Their part of the relationship is to be open and honest with us about the performance and how it's going and to work with us, to help us understand their needs better, when that's required, and to trust us. We still need to set some criteria, some milestones, so they can evaluate our performance, but getting the engagement to the point where we build mutual trust and respect for each other is what truly drives success. If we do that, clients are going to invite us into more business problems and opportunities. And that's what we want: We want long-term relationships. That's what we're interested in, not just one project, one engagement, or one time in and one time out. We're interested in clients for life. Consistently delivering success will ensure that we keep exactly those clients.

A Foundation of Expertise

To offer expertise to your clients, you draw from a number of sources, and you can't use just a few; you have to use all of them. First, you focus on building the expertise along vertical lines. You have to start with a set of leaders who understand a specific industry vertical because they either came from that industry, serviced it for a long time, or have developed relationships in that vertical so they understand the industry. They've been a part of it. From there, the leaders build a consulting team by recruiting talent with similar backgrounds through their work experiences. They must understand the particular work environment and industry needs to have credibility with their clients. Once you have a strong, experienced resource pool, then you define the solutions and the solution teams that are specific to that industry, based on the specific needs of that industry.

When defining solutions, even their names may have industry-specific meanings. For instance, what someone else may call customer relationship management, we call customer care or billing in certain industries. So, in that industry we use a different nomenclature. But it's more than a different nomenclature; there's a unique emphasis and a difference in the way in which we want to go about building the client relationship. It's essential that we understand the solutions and tailor them so that we can deliver a solution to a client that is responsive to the way that vertical goes about its business.

So to build a foundation of expertise, you start with leaders; you build a workforce; and you equip them with methodologies and solutions that are tailored for that marketplace. Then you back them up with knowledge resources – for instance, sample engagement deliverables, white papers, and the experiences we've gained across all of our industry verticals – so that the solutions have been benchmarked against other things, and your professionals have materials to reference. Then you follow that up with an established training program – not just to teach them skills and to teach how those skills apply in that vertical, but also to enable them to keep up with the trends in their verticals, so that they can offer innovation and insight.

Another essential part of this ability to provide insight is understanding what the hot points are and what the technologies are that may influence or affect the industry. As I've stated, it's important to know what the competitive pressures are and what the clients are going through. But I think you also have to back up that understanding with strong alliance relationships. KPMG Consulting has alliance relationships with a veritable Who's Who in the technology business, but in different relationships we target different verticals. For instance, you would take a particular technology to a consumer manufacturing business, where a solid, functional accounting package – a financial system that handles the supply-chain management aspects – would fit very well in their business and in that marketplace. But for a high-tech business where the needs are vastly different – accounting, funds flow management, accounts payable, or plans for establishing an information systems architecture – a different package may be a better answer. So when you're building that vertical competence, you should recognize that you don't take every alliance partner into every vertical. Be aware that there are functional and technical aspects of every alliance partner's products, services, and solutions that fit various verticals differently. They are all part of building the true vertical business.

Finally, it is important to manage the people by verticals, so everyone knows they're in it together, that there is an expertise base, and that you have a clear go-to-market approach. I think the way you set up your profit and loss, manage the business, and set up the rewards structure can all help reinforce this foundation of expertise and these coherent teams. You can't just go hire people who have experience; you have to use that experience to its full advantage and continuously build upon it to enrich your client delivery and keep the business innovative and responsive.

Are All Consulting Companies the Same?

I'm often asked, "Are all these consulting companies the same?" The answer is clearly, "No." But to understand the differences among consulting companies, there are several things you have to examine. Start here, "What is their market focus?" Not all system consultants are focused on the same marketplace. Market focus will or should drive a whole different internal set of solutions, workforces, alliance relationships, and so forth.

The next questions you ask are, "With their specific market focuses, what is their solution set? How have they built that solution set, and how do they take it to market?" Look at their workforce and ask, "What supports that solution in terms of its implementation and execution for the client?" Then look at the very mechanical things inside a company and see how well they stand behind their clients. Ask yourself, "Are they a company that will be there for a long time? Will they support their implementations, standing behind their work? Do they bring new ideas to the table? Do they create new technology that may impact and influence some of the things we've done and things we can do in the future?" I think you have to look at a whole range of things and see who the companies are, across the board, where their focus is, and how good they are at these components.

If, instead, you want to know how to categorize the different companies, I would say there are many different players in our space, the integration space. You have the e-consultants in this space. Their market focus has really been on dot-com concerns and companies that started in the last five to ten years. They're very focused on Web-enabling applications and providing a front-end to the dot-com companies. In addition to e-consultants, big IT services are predominantly outsource businesses. Some of them are hardware businesses; some are software businesses; but they provide a whole array of client services, from hardware to outsourcing to consulting. They're wed to certain hardware and software platforms, and they're very focused on their biggest area of opportunity and revenue – outsourcing.

You have the Big Five companies, and many of their consulting units are spinning off. Most of these Big Five are strong in the applications arena, but some are stronger in systems. Then you have a group of firms that I call the

New Breeds. There are differences even within the New Breeds. In terms of their market focus and solutions, the kind of workforces they've built to support that solution set varies among those firms. Under these criteria, I think we clearly have three major buckets or groups: the e-consultants, the big IT services, and the real, pure integrators. I believe KPMG Consulting is one of only two pure integrators in the public domain.

Managing in a Turbulent Market

The changing economy poses two major challenges for consultants: managing our business and workforce during turbulent times and helping clients manage. We help clients by staying focused on the most important business needs and opportunities a client has and making sure we're working with them up front. We deliver on the client's desired value and results. When the market is cautious and growth is not the same as it was four years ago, clients want to dedicate only the resources and funds that get a real return on investment and help them in a critical need area. Our job is to stay focused on the critical need and on things that really will work and bring the intended results. We are not doing our client any good, unless they ask for it, to try to peddle something else that may be out of that mainstream. I think we have to recognize that all of our clients in all of our industries have different pressures and different concerns, and we have to make sure our approach and solutions recognize these differences.

How do we manage our own business and workforce? I'm a strong believer in sticking to the fundamentals. Our organization would probably prefer that I wasn't, as it is not the most exciting path. I believe, in good times and in bad times, you should stay focused on the fundamentals of business. You can be creative and wild, and being creative but focused is one of the fundamentals of our business.

The fundamentals include: Focus on the client's needs; deliver against those needs; make sure we communicate in response to those needs; make sure we are running our business efficiently with the available resources; and make sure we are investing those resources. Develop the workforce not just for today's needs, but for the needs of tomorrow, as well. Customers will call these fundamentals blocking and tackling, or our bread and butter. I call it being a fundamentalist. The fundamentals are fashionable in both good times and bad times. We tend to overlook them when we're in a boom economy and when everyone talks about growth. Even if you're keeping up with growth, if you're not sticking to the fundamentals, if you're taking advantage of the growth and trying to solidify and streamline your delivery instead of focusing on the client's business problem, you're not going to be there when things turn down. The client won't have confidence in you. I believe we need to stay very focused on the fundamentals – and foremost among them is commitment to our client's success.

Making a Profit When the Economy is Down

Nowhere in the economics book does it say, "If you don't grow, you can't turn a profit." You can still be profitable when the economy is down. You must manage your resources effectively, deploy them where the highest opportunities are, and keep those resources in general synch with your business. When you invest personnel or funds, put them in the most important opportunities, and make them count.

Our company has been growing at a time when no one else's has. The e-consultants have for the most part gone away, and the big IT services have flocked to outsourcing, and everyone really seems to want to abandon what I called the systems integration space. We didn't abandon it. We stuck with it, and we grew. That's not to say that we are not having tougher times in some sectors. The national service sector, which we have been very public about, has not been as robust as some of our other business units. Even in that area, we can still be profitable, just by keeping our bookings consistent, focusing our investments, and delivering on the promises we have made to clients.

Further, if we are gaining market share by adding clients, our total revenue may not be going up, but we may be able to gain presence with certain clients or marketplaces where we couldn't before. We can then leverage them later. Downturns in the economy present these opportunities, as well as others, for us to be challenged, to face the challenge, and to be rewarded for having done so – not just monetary rewards, but also recognition and promotion opportunities and opportunities to fulfill one's own personal goals and commitments. I think you can get a win-win even in the tough times. I feel very strongly that if you've taken advantage of the tough times, you'll be better positioned when things improve.

Advice for Business and Leadership

Take care of your people. Develop them; nurture them; and move them forward, because their success is your success. I would say a great deal of my personal success has come because I've been able to pick, recruit, mentor, and turn over much of the business to some very bright people, some of whom are probably brighter than I am. These professionals are able to catapult the business forward. To the extent that you can do that, you are going to be better off, and you will have those people to turn to. You will help ensure your own and the future success of the business.

The best leaders anywhere, whether they're government officials, business leaders, or sports people, are those individuals who understand the importance of people. They are very fair in how they treat people and how they want their business to treat other businesses. It's not just person-to-person; it's organization-to-organization, too. Being fair-minded is very important. It drives your culture and your success.

Taking Risks

Every time we take on a new client, it's a risk because we're not familiar with that client. We may know the client's business problem, and we may understand the environment they face. But we haven't yet worked across the table with them day-in and day-out, over the long periods of a contract and reached the end of a contract. In these cases, we do prospective client evaluations to take a look at the new client and the scenario we are entering, so we can really get a sense of whether or not we can meet the client's expectations. We owe it to clients to tell them up front when there are things we're concerned about, even if it's a competitive situation.

In these evaluations we have an analytical tool that puts some of that risk on the table. We can discuss things with our client and, if they see things differently than we do, make a conscious decision to perhaps just stop the relationship. It may be the right outcome for both of us in the long term.

I've explained that every time we sign a new client, which is probably every day, we're taking a risk. I think the way to protect against the risk is to establish some processes so that risk is one of the first things considered and certainly an element that is always considered. The prospective client evaluation has to be completed and signed by one of our risk-managing directors, who will give it a second check and balance. It forces us to be to be very deliberate in our thinking.

For every business decision we make, we need to think about the risks. We have to imbed certain processes that force risk to be considered in every decision – not just considering it, but making sure we have a response game plan. Once we've identified those risks, we need to balance or react to each risk that manifests itself. We do that in our decision-making processes. Does it slow the decision-making process down by a day or three or six? It could, but it is the prudent thing to do.

Even some projects with existing clients pose risks. It may be one candidate who has strong technical skills, and another has great communication skills. If for this client, our team is strong enough technically, we may need a communications person to be the lead on this specific engagement. We need to see that the risk of getting out of synch in this situation is the communication. Since risk is something that's imbedded in every decision we make, we have to make it a conscious part of the decision process, and we have to make sure we've been up front about it. We have imbedded processes to facilitate that with checks and balances.

Keeping the Edge

The only way to keep your edge is to be out in the marketplace, seeing the real pressures people face every day. People inside KPMG Consulting would probably say I'm a very good administrator: I understand the business, understand the fundamentals, and make sure all the elements of the business talk to each other and keep moving. But being a good administrator doesn't give me an edge. If I'm not out there with our professionals or clients, seeing what affects them, I'm going to lose my edge. So I have to spend a certain amount of time and a lot of my thought in their framework, inside their positions, either through dialogue, engagement reviews, or meetings with our people and our clients. But as I said earlier, this is the enjoyable part.

The Future of Consulting

The fundamentals of locking on a client's business problem are not going to change in the next decade. Clients will still have businesses and business priorities, and they will still need information. The validity and accuracy of the information are getting faster and faster, and the way virtual organizations are created won't significantly change.

I think technology will step up the pace, adding new wrinkles and new solutions. Technology brings us closer to operating virtually and enables consulting professionals to work remotely with clients more than we ever could before. All of this enables globalization, which I think is going to be very dominant in years to come. We're focused on the Global 2000 companies, but any company in the world is global. Either their customer base is global, or their vendor base is global. Most companies do some transactions outside their regional or national borders. We need to operate globally ourselves and assist our clients as they face similar globalization needs, helping them achieve results and success without boundaries.

In the past it seemed easy to enter this profession. The perception was you put up a sign in your window that said, "I'm a consultant," and you were in business. I don't think that's fair to the state of the profession. I think consulting, particularly for the global companies, is a very sophisticated business. Organizations put a lot on the line with the consultants they choose. I believe that those consulting companies that are able to deliver real value on a sustained basis will be the ones that are still here five years from now. The marketplace learned that a new technology plus a new consulting firm does not necessarily result in staying power for the firm. The staying power comes from being a sophisticated business made up of experienced people who can provide lasting results.

Randolph C. Blazer is chairman and CEO of KPMG Consulting, Inc. He manages over 10,200 employees within six industry lines of business around the world. KPMG Consulting provides Internet integration services, which include strategy, e-branding and design, web architecture, integration, technology enabling, and hosting/outsourcing. Mr. Blazer is based in the headquarters office in Tysons Corner, VA.

In 1977, Mr. Blazer joined KPMG LLP as a consulting professional in the Washington, D.C., office. In 1991, he was named partner-in-charge of KPMG's Public Sector Consulting group. In 1997, he was named a member of a two-person executive team that directed all KPMG Consulting services. In February 2000, Mr. Blazer helped incorporate the consulting group into KPMG Consulting, LLC.

Mr. Blazer has more than 25 years of experience in strategic business planning, performance management, process reengineering, and large-scale systems development support to major government and commercial clients. His client experience includes work with federal agencies and departments, research universities, government contractors, and major federal system acquisition programs.

Prior to joining KPMG, Mr. Blazer served as a captain in the United States Army.

Mr. Blazer received his MBA from the University of Kentucky and his BA in economics from Western Maryland College.

WORKING AT THE INTERFACE OF TECHNOLOGY AND BUSINESS

PAMELA MCNAMARA

Arthur D. Little, Inc.

Chief Executive Officer

Rewards of Consulting

In 1998, research at a major pharmaceutical company showed that one of its products, which had originally been developed for the treatment of breast cancer, could also be effective in the prevention of breast cancer. Since breast cancer is a major health concern, the company immediately realized the importance of getting the product to market as quickly as possible, a process that typically takes up to 18 months. The firm contacted Arthur D. Little, Inc., to help re-launch the product to take advantage of its new indications as soon as possible. This was not an unusual assignment, but the goal of completing it in just eight to ten weeks was challenging.

We immediately assembled an interdisciplinary team of about 16 people, half from ADL and half from the client company, rolled up our sleeves, and jumped in, feeling more than a little daunted by the technical, financial, regulatory, and marketing barriers before us. The project was dubbed "Moonshot" because the prospects for success seemed to be well captured by the old expression about the impossibility of "shooting the moon."

All of us were driven by this extraordinary challenge. Not only was there the immediate practical business goal to urge us on, but it was also clear to us all that getting this product to market would save lives. We worked together day and night, isolated in a hot, cramped building, far from the company headquarters, that we called the LEM, after the Lunar Excursion Module from the Apollo moon-landing program. We brainstormed; we conducted analyses; we argued and compromised; we developed plans; we took actions; and we drank lots of coffee.

And we succeeded. The product, one of the first drugs to be used in the prevention of any form of cancer, made it to the market in just eight weeks.

For me, this project captures all that is best about the consulting profession. It was an extraordinary, multifaceted challenge; we had an exceptional team of client representatives, together with our own players; we learned a lot; and we made a real difference – not only for the company, but also for society as a whole. Of course, not all of these elements show up to the same degree in all assignments, but they are always there in some combination.

The problems and opportunities I've worked on have really made a difference to our clients and, in most cases, to society and our economy. The central purpose of consulting, after all, is to make a difference. We are called in only when there is a challenge, a need to change or innovate, not to run day-to-day operations.

In the process, we must listen and learn, because that is central to meeting the needs of the client. But just as importantly, our ability to build on each experience – drawing upon our deep industry, business, and technology experience – is the cornerstone of future success and the essence of professional satisfaction.

I can't overstate the importance of teamwork to job satisfaction. There are few more personally rewarding experiences than working together with a group of others toward a common goal. Not only is collaborating with team members in our firm, as well as with client staff, personally satisfying, but whoever said that two heads are better than one was right on the mark. One plus one plus one equals six in this business.

The best career advice I ever received was to focus on what's most important to me – what I hold dear and where I want to make a difference. Fortunately for me, there has been a confluence of those elements in consulting. It has been particularly rewarding for me, therefore, to be able to blend my personal and business lives, focusing on what I care about most. This delivers real results – financial and strategic value – to our clients.

Challenges Facing Women in Consulting

Of course, there are many more men than women in consulting. And to some extent, there can be different expectations for women, partially because of the different roles we have traditionally played in society as wives and mothers, for example. Consulting is inherently an international profession, and values and expectations can vary widely across nations and cultures. Ultimately, however, it doesn't matter whether you're a man or a woman, particularly as women are becoming more and more successful worldwide. Even in countries where there are still barriers to full acceptance of women, there tends to be an understanding that women are playing leading roles in many societies. For me, the key has been not to dwell on the possibility of barriers and drawbacks, but to focus instead on developing the competence, confidence, and professionalism required to do the job.

To be successful in this business, you have to stick to the important basics of knowing your territory, delivering profits, challenging your clients to think about the tough issues, maintaining your integrity, and paying close attention to the people aspects of consulting. You have to listen well, determine how to make sure the results are owned by your clients, and follow through on implementing. Those are skills I've learned from both men and women professionals. I think the consulting profession is one in which the best players bring those characteristics to the table, and I've worked with both men and women who exemplify those qualities.

Good mentors can make a great deal of difference. At ADL, I've been fortunate to have some fabulous mentors over time, and a number of them have been women. When I joined the firm back in the early eighties, we had, relatively speaking, a large number of women professionals in the senior ranks, and I can think of quite a few of them who made a difference in coaching me, as well as in providing inspiration as role models in the organization.

At the same time, I must make it clear that not all of my mentors and role models have been women, nor should they be. What matters most in this business is how to deliver excellent results and bring in new business. There is much to be learned from both men and women who have succeeded in this profession.

Differences Among Consulting Firms

Each consulting firm has its own corporate culture or "personality" that arises from such key variables as its business focus, approach, organization, history, and even its size. In the interest of full disclosure, my views are heavily colored by having spent virtually my entire career at Arthur D. Little. I have done so because of the particular culture of this place, which I have found to be both personally and professionally rewarding.

Many companies have been very successful in focusing on specific functional domains, such as supply-chain management, accounting and financial operations, or information technology, for example. These firms, many of which are quite large and may embrace a range of specialties, have people who have expertise in these particular arenas, and most have developed rigorous methodologies that work well for them.

ADL is something of an exception in that its chief business focus is at the intersection of business and the diverse range of technologies that drive innovation in our society. In today's business press, "technology" has been appropriated to refer specifically to information technology, including such elements as telecommunications, networks, software, computers, and the Internet. But at ADL, we embrace technologies ranging from information technology and its underlying field of electronics, all the way to biotech, materials, energy, and food technology.

This focus arises from the firm's historic capabilities in research and development. Throughout the last century, ADL was responsible for the development of such innovations as the first iso-octane, which was later adopted as the antiknock gasoline standard; a process for making blown glass fibers, which led to Fiberglas™; the first computerized inventory control package for IBM; the design of the NASDAQ stock exchange system now in London and Tokyo; the first fiber-optic interactive cable television system near Osaka, Japan; and the development of environmental auditing.

We continue to develop products in our own laboratories, as well as in partnership with others. Current examples range from a low-fat ice cream that incorporates fish oil, which is associated with significant health benefits, to a novel medical device that can identify the previously undetectable areas in coronary arteries most likely to cause heart attacks, and a system that allows organizations to monitor and manage energy use and greenhouse gas emissions across all operations.

An explosion of research and development in industry and universities increasingly formed the basis of new business opportunities throughout the 20th century. Accordingly, the company expanded its capabilities to embrace the broader strategic and day-to-day management implications of work in a broad range of technical fields. It has also embraced the issues of venture capital and start-up management required to bring ideas and innovations to the market.

In a broad sense, all businesses today are high-technology businesses. There is hardly a business decision in any industry that does not have a central technological component. Product development, manufacturing processes, finance, information systems, environmental compliance, packaging, product distribution, service delivery, market analysis, and even management itself, as well as organizational processes, have all been – and will continue to be – transformed by technological developments.

This hands-on technological focus, which has yielded specific products and processes, has given a decidedly practical and creative feel to ADL's culture and its work. The nature of the tasks we undertake, and our approach to them, require that we work in close partnership with our clients, whether we are developing and introducing a new product or restructuring an organization.

This approach, and the resulting culture, are reinforced by the fact that we often hire people with extensive industry experience. We employ engineers and scientists with expertise in these technologies, as well as experts in the classic functional areas, such as strategy and operations. We also seek people who have actually worked in operations in companies for five to ten or more years before they joined ADL. The idea is to assemble a multi-disciplinary staff that can draw on industry experience, as well as the wide range of areas of expertise that may be required to address the challenges our clients face. This, of course, reflects the reality of business challenges: The great majority of them are inherently multidisciplinary.

In ADL's Health Industries Practice, for example, our goal is to work with clients to drive business and technology innovation at the frontiers of health and medicine. Accordingly, our business model for that practice brings together expertise and resources in technology development, commercialization, and venturing, as well as consulting. It is the interplay among these core elements that provides the driving force for innovation in that area.

The fundamental approach of assembling individuals who can help a company through the entire process of innovation, from concept to commercialization, creates a diverse culture at ADL, and a demanding one. But the rewards are commensurate with the effort required to meet the demands.

The Art and Craft of Consulting

Consulting is a creative process. At the base level, of course, there are a variety of underlying skills and methodologies that support the process, but true success ultimately depends on finding out how to build on them, to go beyond them and the latest management "fads" to develop the novel ideas and insights that provide real value to a client.

The key to achieving success lies in what some might call the "golden rules" of consulting:

Understand your niche.
Hire the best people.
Build a strong team.
Involve the client in the solution.
Communicate.

Understand your niche.

Every consulting firm must first understand what makes it different from any other, especially in a crowded and highly competitive market. This understanding forms the basis for every aspect of the business, from new strategic directions to hiring and marketing. It also sets bounds on the type and variety of cases undertaken. ADL, for example, has set itself apart by its firm grounding in technology, as I've mentioned.

Within that context, a firm must provide itself with the latitude to keep strengthening its position by developing complementary areas of competency, for example, either in response to – or even better, in anticipation of – changes in the marketplace. It may also be necessary to phase out some competencies as the market evolves to keep the business focused on the client needs that the firm is best able to meet. This process of renewal, weeding out unprofitable capabilities, and developing new ones within the context of the overall business focus, must be continuous because the needs of client organizations are changing continuously as technical, economic, political, environmental, and social forces shape our society.

In the struggle to carve out a niche, consulting firms have sometimes been criticized for their role in creating or encouraging "fads" in business and management, such as re-engineering and total quality management. In truth, many of these approaches are little more than a repackaging of the same core human and organizational insights wrapped in slightly different terminology and processes. The underlying message here is that there can be real value to consulting and, as long as it leads quickly to a clear mutual understanding of the problems at hand and to a viable solution, the path to get there is of lesser importance.

Hire the best people.

There's an adage that says, "When it comes to hiring, 'good enough' never is." A consulting firm's chief asset, indeed its only real asset, is its people. Assembling and developing that asset is the cornerstone of success. Knowledge and experience are threshold requirements. Many consultants can deliver them, but that's not good enough. The critical difference – the difference that makes successful consulting an art – is in the people skills. It is the combination of being able to listen well and to frame a client's challenges accurately and concisely at the beginning, and then to manage those challenges with clear expectations as the relationship evolves – which it always does.

I take notice of individual consultants who have great people skills, high energy, the ability to make things happen, the drive to achieve tangible goals and get things done, and openness and flexibility in working with others. They're skilled at drawing out the ideas of others. They're clear in setting and managing goals and expectations, managing flexibility, and managing change. They persevere. We deal with a lot of the uncertainty facing our clients in dynamic and challenging circumstances. The people who are best at working with this uncertainty are the ones who stand out. The threshold is having the expertise and the content knowledge – and we need that for certain, especially given our company's business model. But it's that added value that's above and beyond the threshold that makes individuals stand out.

Finally, top consultants thrive on challenging others and being challenged. These individuals are contrary when they need to be, and they're not afraid to take strong positions.

Further, they put their positions out on the table in a fully candid and transparent way, so we know where they're coming from. Sometimes this sets the stage for conflict – but it's conflict that is always based on integrity and that often serves as the basis for a creative edge.

Build a strong team.

Teambuilding is essential to our art because it is the true foundation of innovation and creativity. There are two principal reasons for this.

First, a great majority of real business challenges are interdisciplinary or multifaceted. Starting up a new operation, for example, may involve expertise in product development, manufacturing technology, strategic management, and marketing, to name just a few. In assessing the dimensions of a problem, it is crucial to determine the kinds of expertise and experience that will be required to provide a realistic solution in a timely fashion, and to bring together a group of individuals who can meet those requirements.

Second, successful teams are a constant reminder that the whole is greater than the sum of its parts. Properly organized and managed, groups of people drive each other to be faster and more creative in arriving at a solution to a problem. Team members coach one another, challenge solutions, and remain unsatisfied until they know they have reached the top. That's the art, and it makes the difference.

In the most successful situations – the cancer prevention product launch is a clear example – the team members from both the client organization and our company are so intensively focused on the process that individual credit doesn't matter. There's an ongoing, high-intensity, and highly creative dynamic of tackling what needs to be done and of constantly evolving interim objectives, while keeping the ultimate objective clear.

Involve the client in the solution.

In the end, the client must fully understand and embrace the results of any consulting work. The best way to ensure that happens is to forge a working partnership with the client. The overall goal is to work not so much *for* a client, but *with* the client.

This process begins by listening. There is no faster way to win the confidence of another party than to listen to that party's needs, interests, demands, and concerns, and then to show that you have been listening by framing the challenge at hand in a way that reflects and addresses all its aspects. We bring to the table a deep understanding of not only the client industry, but also of other industries from which best practices can be drawn, as well as the business and technology operations – in short, we know how to make things work. It is crucial to blend these skills in the early stages to set the context, but it remains important throughout the entire project.

In many cases, it is best to build a team that specifically involves client staff, as well as consulting team staff. This guarantees that the all-important client perspective and expertise is available throughout the evolving course of a project. After all, any client knows the operational details of the business better than an outsider does. Moreover, client team members must become the "owners" of the end results, with a full understanding of the short-term and long-term implications for the firm.

Again, people skills are vital. It is important to recognize the different strengths and weaknesses in individuals, on both the client staff and our consulting team staff, so that there's a good match and fit with the task at hand and with the ongoing relationship beyond it. And we have to give all the individuals involved opportunities to stretch themselves, to go above and beyond what's expected. I look on this as a dynamic process, like a living organism, that takes a lot of care and feeding. We check in constantly with the various players on the client staff, and nurture and coach our consulting team.

Communicate.

Integral with involving the client and building effective teams is communication. In client surveys conducted at ADL, communication is often cited as the most important aspect of a relationship, either as the key to a success or as an area for improvement.

Excellent communication begins with a clear mutual understanding of the goals and approach to any project. It continues with regular updates to establish and manage expectations, an ongoing exchange of information between parties – including updates from both the client and the consulting firm – and presentation of the results. More often than not, the action of summarizing progress and reporting results actually stimulates and enriches the process of synthesizing those results, leading to further insights in clearer directions.

Perhaps more to the point, communication is critically important because of the dynamic and evolving nature of most consulting projects. During the course of implementing a strategy, it is not uncommon for a variety of aspects to change, including economic conditions, market conditions, operational results, political developments, and emerging technologies. Given that consulting is also a discovery process, it is not uncommon for the project team to uncover entirely new aspects of a challenge in the midst of addressing it. This requires close communication among team members and the sponsoring client to keep all apprised of developments, frame expectations, and make adjustments toward revised goals.

Relationship Management

Although ADL has a broad spectrum of relationships with companies of many sizes and from a wide variety of industries, the firms that tend to achieve the greatest benefits are those with whom we have long-term relationships that cut across more than one of our areas of expertise.

A consulting firm is, in fact, designed to be complementary in nature to a typical business operation. Most companies hire individuals with the particular areas of expertise required to manage the routine aspects of their business effectively. This can include research and product development, as well as strategy and planning and day-to-day management. At ADL, we assemble a staff of individuals with the broad range of relevant areas of expertise required to help a client change or innovate, providing industry-wide, as well as cross-industry, perspective, specialized management and organizational knowledge, and familiarity with a broad variety of technologies and the dynamics of start-up operations.

Given the wide spectrum of possibilities, it is impractical for client companies to maintain such a staff.

In a new relationship, or if we're working with a client again after a long absence, we do our homework. We determine whether this client organization is a good fit with our strengths, our direction, and our portfolio of services. We have set a goal, for example, to work with some of the leading biotechnology players in the health and pharmaceutical industries. So we've developed further capabilities and connections that will keep us at the front edge of innovation in those fields. When we start working with a client organization, we already understand what its greatest needs are and where those needs have the best fit with us.

Whether we have had a long-term relationship and many engagements with a client, or we are starting a new relationship, we focus on the specific needs of the client. In this process, we frame the needs so that we understand the client's objectives, what the client is able to address on its own, where the gaps are, and the relative importance of filling each of those gaps. We estimate the timing and then determine explicitly what to tackle, how to get it done, and how to manage expectations, evaluate results, measure the value, and satisfy the client's defined needs.

A key goal in developing a relationship for the longer term is to build a true partnership. Even in shorter-term projects, it is important to work in close conjunction with a client firm, melding perspectives and areas of expertise from each party, and building both formal and informal lines of communication. In both the short term and the long term, the partnership model greatly enhances the effectiveness of a relationship. Each party develops a deeper appreciation for the other; communication improves; and a stronger sense of mutual buy-in emerges.

Teamwork is critical in forming and cementing these relationships. Once we have worked jointly on a project in teams made up of client representatives, as well as ADL staff, we develop the mutual understanding and respect that allows us to move on to more – and more varied – engagements.

For the clients with whom we have a longer history of engagements, we make sure we help them with their technology and product portfolios and with the new growth arenas they're charting or developing. And in some cases, we'll also help clients form alliances with some of the hot new leading technology players, extending their relationships to a broader network.

Once we start working with a client, we have some consistent ways to frame the client's challenges. First, there is timing. We determine how important the need is to the client's near-term or longer-term strategic priorities. We also consider where the problem lies – within a defined business or operating unit, across multiple groups of the client's organization, or even potentially outside the enterprise. We work to understand the dynamics and complexity of who has to be involved to achieve results. We consider which elements of our capabilities will be needed: Is this a strategy or an organizational set of issues? Is it more operational, or is it related to R&D management or product management or innovation management, or maybe environmental management? What are the elements of the problem that might lend themselves to product development technologies?

We also size up the problem in terms of where we might find sources for good ideas and solutions. We develop a clear understanding of the expertise we have on our team. Certainly, we have staff who know the industry domain, whether it is healthcare, energy, chemicals, or telecommunications, for example. But we may also have staff who have actually worked in this client organization itself and who understand its dynamics and culture. In many instances, we bring in staff to help discover where there might be solution ideas from leaders in other industries who have already been working to solve the kinds of problem our client is facing.

Maintaining the Creative Edge

Because of the accelerating pace of change in the world business community, in the international research community, and in society in general, developing and maintaining expertise is a constant challenge for a consulting firm. The intellectual and practical satisfaction of maintaining that edge, however, is one of the great rewards of the profession.

Most consultants tend to read voraciously, seeking new ideas and insights as they emerge around the world. Because of the many dimensions of the problems we address, it is important to read both broadly and deeply. Being an international firm is a real plus in this regard, because it allows staff to keep abreast of trends and developments in markets throughout the world through clients, colleagues, and research.

Many consultants also write for leading industry, business, and professional publications, as well, including ADL's own publications, such as *Prism*, which highlights the achievements and thinking of our staff, as well as those of our client partners. In addition, it is not uncommon for firms to prepare white papers on key topics and trends in industry, technology, and society. It has often been said that writing is thinking. And indeed, the action of writing white papers and articles is important because it is an opportunity to synthesize the broader lessons emerging from our work and to keep our own name associated with thought leadership in the key fields that are important to us strategically.

In truth, every case a consulting firm undertakes is a learning experience. A key function at many firms is knowledge management – the organization and cataloguing of case experiences for use as a proprietary resource in future cases. It is essential for an organization to capture the essence of its experience and insights in a form that remains within the company in the inevitable event of staff turnover.

Staff turnover is common throughout the consulting profession as individuals pursue new or different challenges at other firms and in other industries. Obviously, this turnover is sometimes inconvenient, but at the same time, a minimum level of turnover (say, 10 to 15 percent) is critical to renewing and enriching the talent pool with high performers. It is also often a net gain for a company, since it brings in new ideas, new experiences, and new areas of expertise. Regularly bringing in fresh faces and fresh minds helps keep an organization on its toes and provides opportunities for it to adapt quickly to a changing world.

Networking is a must. One of the key "people skills" consulting staff must have is the ability to maintain a strong network of relationships with other firms, alumni, universities, journalists, and others. Staff must stay deeply in touch with the marketplace, talking and listening to a variety of companies, not all of whom are our clients. Such a network keeps you abreast of current thinking, and it can also be used as a resource for advice, perspective, contacts, and assistance.

When you hire a good consultant, you're getting that individual and his or her range of networks with business and academia that keep fresh ideas and fresh perspectives flowing. Through these contacts, consultants learn; they absorb information; they see patterns; and they "put it together" in new ways, leading to new insights and approaches. It takes tenacity and discipline to make those calls, but it is necessary to keep checking in with those networks. The hunger for learning what's out there and hearing what others are doing and challenging what others are thinking is a key part of the consulting dynamic.

A whole host of collaborative tools are now appearing that help consulting firms maintain their edge. A number of firms, including an ADL spin-off, have developed Internet-based tools for complex project management that allow disparate groups to work together in real-time on multifaceted projects. These software packages make it easier for teams to set goals, share information, report progress, synthesize data, and respond dynamically to inevitable changes and new developments during the course of a project.

There are other practices, as well, that help a consulting firm stay sharp. Training is important, of course, as it is a regular and formal channel designed to keep a flow of new learning and experience coming into the company, and it serves to spread our experience to new staff, as well as those rising through career stages. From time to time, we also run best-practice surveys, attend meetings, conduct a number of our own business roundtables for executives, run workshops for our clients and others, and stay in touch with universities, occasionally sponsoring some of their initiatives and research.

Finally, client feedback is a crucial aspect of the process of staying at the competitive edge. As many firms do, ADL maintains a well-defined process for soliciting and assessing the client's views of our performance. This presents a clearer picture, not only of what we are doing right, but also of what we can do better.

Leadership and Management in Turbulent Times

We now live in a world where all times are turbulent. This is either the first great lesson of the 21st century, or the last great lesson of the previous century. With the accelerating pace of economic, social, political, environmental, and technological developments in today's world, change has become the norm for all businesses. This, of course, presents a host of challenges and opportunities, both for consulting firms and for our clients, as we seek to understand the nature of emerging developments and how to either accommodate them or leverage them in an innovative fashion in the marketplace.

Change – advising about it and managing it – is the particular province of consulting firms, but our own organizations and strategies can be buffeted by it as much as those of our clients can. A particular challenge for our industry is to stay a step ahead in the management of our own businesses, as well as in advising others. As the economy goes through its cycles, advances in science and engineering open up promising business opportunities; new businesses and industries emerge; and more mature industries struggle to adapt or reinvent themselves, we must be prepared to assess the importance of these changes for our clients.

A few key elements, summarized below, can help a company maintain a steady course in the midst of the push and shove of today's competitive marketplace.

Leadership

In becoming a senior leader at ADL, it has been important for me to embrace the differences between management and management consulting. After all, running a company, even a consulting company, is not the same as running a consulting project. As I mentioned, the skills and insights of consultants are complementary to those of the clients we serve. Consultants provide the knowledge and experience in management and technology required to help firms innovate, adapt to change, or anticipate change. This requires both broad and deep context in technological developments, industrial practice, company operations, local and national economies, and organizational change. Just as the best coaches in sports were not necessarily the best players, the best managers are not always the best management consultants.

Nonetheless, the lessons of consulting have much to bring to the task of leadership as we face the challenges and opportunities of a turbulent world. Applying our own insights and experience to ourselves, however, is easier said than done for organizations more accustomed to dispensing advice than receiving it. Moreover, consulting firms have an inherently outward professional focus, concentrating with such energy on client challenges that internal needs may be neglected.

An overriding philosophy of mine is that a leader should be the servant to the organization as a whole. The leader should serve in a manner so that the group as a whole does better – advancing, achieving its goals, and promoting good organizational health and vibrancy.

As in other businesses, a leader of a consulting firm must have a vision, both personally and for the organization. You must be deliberate and effective in execution; and you must have strong people skills. You need to be good at both listening and building consensus as you're building a team. But you also have to recognize when decisions have to be made at the expense of consensus.

Shared Values

Successful teams go through the hard work of understanding the characteristics, qualities, and shared beliefs inherent in the work they are doing, and the goals they're striving to achieve. They agree on the roles, the expectations, the contributions of the team members, how they relate to each other, and how they participate as a team. And they have a common major goal or vision that will stretch their capabilities, and the flexibility to do what it takes, playing full out, to reach it.

ADL's shared values, which have emerged from our long history, include a genuine drive to innovate, a passion for excellence, a spirit of collegiality, and a commitment to integrity. These values have consistently formed the underpinnings of our approaches to the marketplace as they have evolved over time. More to the point, they have been vital to the company's success over the years, and they are a crucial part of what attracts and holds employees. The company has been able to preserve and institutionalize the core values that have sustained us through many changes and, indeed, have become part of the ADL brand.

Balancing Strengths

Smart consulting organizations maintain a portfolio of clients and industries, so that at any time, there is a mix of industry sectors and client organizations that can help the firm through normal client business cycles. It is also useful to maintain a range of services, some of which may be more appropriate for helping a client through tighter times and some of which can help a company take advantage of better times.

We have deep strengths in both the energy sector and the telecom sector, for example. A few years ago, when the energy sector was having a tough time, we did a lot of work to help our oil and gas clients solve some of their problems. With most of those problems resolved, there were some lulls with those clients, and we redirected our focus. Then the telecommunications business started on its massive growth cycle. But in the last several months, the telecommunications sector has been facing some rough times, and we've shifted our focus again to those clients with current needs we can meet. At the same time, we've had very strong energy business because the energy sector has been growing and once again becoming highly profitable.

Balancing strengths is inherently a dynamic process. Not only do businesses go through cycles, but the underlying technologies driving innovation spring up, mature, and fade away.

A balance of strengths is also crucial to the client relationship-building process, which remains important at all times, whether the company is doing well or tightening its belt, and whether we are engaged in a specific project or not. By keeping in touch with firms at all times, we can keep aware of the challenges they are facing and offer our assistance where our current or emerging capabilities overlap their needs.

Setting Business Goals

Goal setting is a constant iterative process. Setting goals for the company is an activity we periodically refresh through think sessions and work sessions with our top staff. We have brought in not only the top leadership team, but also the most provocative thinkers in the business as part of our periodic strategy, budget, and operations planning. We cascade these plans and goals through the business in a way that invites input and response, a process that enriches the vision and direction of the company. It also helps set the context for, and promote clearer understanding of, more specific goals, measurable objectives, and the metrics we use to track the business.

Communication

We constantly reinforce goals and objectives – and our values and accomplishments, as well – in our communications to staff. The head of global communications for our company works very closely with me and with our business leaders to frame not only our internal communications to staff, but also our external communications, along the major dimensions of our business strategy, operations, and achievements. Ours is a people business, and we are constantly evolving, refreshing, and communicating our plans and seeking input from staff. Keeping open channels of communication, both formal and informal, is essential in a business that relies on the cooperation and participation of a network of partners and associates.

Taking Risks

Taking risks is the key to anticipating the future. Although it is essential to have dependable, healthy practices to count on, we must also take risks to push out ahead into new domains or growth areas. Some of these gambles will not pay off as well as others, if at all. But a considered strategy of risk-taking can go a long way toward promoting long-term success.

For example, in the early to mid-1900s, ADL invented the field of flavor analysis, which led to a significant portion of our business. We were also the first to develop the concept of environmental auditing in the 1980s. More recently, the firm has been active in creating and spinning off companies to capitalize on ideas generated in-house or in partnership with other firms.

Hiring is another form of risk-taking. In hiring individuals, you are often looking for people who, given a free rein, can go the extra mile in developing novel approaches to addressing client challenges. Similarly, it is important to maintain enough flexibility in a consulting organization to allow individuals to test new ideas, approaches, or markets. Such experimentation can pose risks, but it can also lead to better job satisfaction for the innovators, better results for the clients, and new opportunities for the company.

The Future of Consulting

In 1886, Arthur D. Little, who dropped out of the Massachusetts Institute of Technology after just three years, founded a company with the idea that industry may, from time to time, need help in exploiting the potential of emerging technologies in their businesses. And indeed, technological advances – in everything from plastics and pharmaceuticals to computers, electronics, and new approaches to manufacturing – formed the cornerstone of a vast variety of business innovations in the 20th century in virtually every industry.

Today, more than ever, technology remains the cornerstone of business innovation, with an increasing pace of developments in a growing range of areas, including semiconductors, biotechnology, telecommunications, renewable energy, and advanced materials, to name just a few. These advances have had, and continue to have, major implications for strategy, organization, product mixes, marketing approaches, and new business development in industries ranging from retail to energy resources. This accelerating pace of change, coupled with increasing worldwide competition, means that there is a growing need for business to figure out how to make use of these advances – some of them happening in their own labs – to gain an edge in their existing operations or to move in entirely new directions.

Information technology, with its exceptional potential for widespread application in business through computers and software, was the first technology broadly embraced as a specialty by the consulting industry. In the late 1990s, an enormous new consulting market burst on the scene to help companies exploit the power of telecommunications and the Internet, an outgrowth of information technology. Promises and expectations outpaced reality, however, leading to a collapse of the market and casting a pall over the entire consulting industry.

This dot-com bubble, however, underscores the strong need for organizations that can cut through the hype to provide realistic and substantive advice on the potential of emerging developments. There is no question that the Internet and telecommunications advances have transformed business worldwide, and that they will continue to do so, but reaping the rewards of this transformation will require a keener understanding of a broad combination of underlying technical, management, and communications issues.

Many of the dot-com firms that sprang up to exploit this technology had a great deal of technical expertise, but not enough knowledge and experience in business and management to be able to capitalize effectively, or to help their clients capitalize effectively. On the other side, many client companies grasped the upside business potential, but hired the dot-com firms to help them because they didn't have the technical expertise to exploit it. The combination, fueled by bright expectations, was a disaster.

One of the legacies of the dot-com phenomenon is that companies are looking for the depth and quality found in the more mainstream consulting firms. Moreover, they are looking for consultants with more solid business experience. The days of freshly minted MBAs advising corporate giants are in the past as today's clients seek consultants who have had the time to hone their skills and insights both in industry and in the consulting business.

As we continue into the 21st century, it will be ever more important for companies to work with consulting firms to sift through the burgeoning array of emerging technologies to determine which are commensurate with their goals, and how they can best fit into their business. Technology, after all, is not an end in itself, but a means to an end. The real goal is to incorporate it as an appropriate element in an overall business or strategic plan.

Especially exciting will be finding ways we can move technology applications from one arena to another to enable us to open new frontiers. It is interesting to note that it was not the makers of vacuum tubes who recognized the potential of semiconductors – it was entirely new companies. And when biotech burst on the scene in the mid-1970s from university labs, it caught many established pharmaceutical companies by surprise. Applications of computers and semiconductor chips are expanding into new areas on an almost daily basis. And information technology is a crucial element of such emerging fields as bioinformatics and proteomics. The ability to harness those opportunities will depend on people with deep expertise in those areas and who also have the skills – people skills and implementation skills – to work with multiple, diverse groups to make it happen.

We are going to see more and more companies realize they can't solve all their problems by themselves. We've seen a myriad of merger and acquisition waves in every industry, as well as different patterns of alliances and partnerships. Many have achieved the minimum, but overall, results have been disappointing. There will be a lot of new effort to work across enterprises to harness existing skills, insights, innovations, and technologies and to explore ways to chart the path for turning these relationships into exciting, valuable, and profitable business propositions.

More broadly, a key challenge to consulting firms will be to deliver clear value to their clients. Particularly in tighter economic times and times of mounting competition, client companies want to ensure that they receive significant benefits for the money they spend on consulting. Today is not a time for fads, but for results.

In the past, a company might have been able to make a promise to a client on the basis of image and reputation. But today we are being challenged to be more and more explicit around managing and demonstrating that value proposition. Our ability to deliver on that value proposition with assurance is based both in hard economics and in the quality and depth of the personal relationships that make up the partnership between a consulting firm and a client.

The demand for more substance and accountability reinforces the need for more consulting firms to develop working partnerships with clients, getting immersed in implementation, as well as analysis. To accommodate the complexity inherent in business challenges, these partnerships may involve other parties with complementary expertise as well. The "arms-length" relationships of the past are likely to become less prevalent.

It is increasingly clear that what may be a new and fresh insight today, and might in previous years have had a half-life of three to six months, can now be out of date in a matter of weeks. Those who will succeed are the individuals or firms that are the best at anticipating the next set of changes, adapting to them, working effectively across enterprises and many types of people, putting ideas into practice, being accountable for results, and moving on to meet the next set of changes. Successful consultants will be able to help client companies place their bets and take their options.

There's no single answer or approach in a world such as this. The winners will be the ones who have the flexibility and the creativity to shape their approaches to meet each demand – even as they are grasping the changing needs and the emerging opportunities.

A consultant with Arthur D. Little for 21 years, Pamela McNamara became CEO in August 2001. As acting CEO, McNamara cut corporate costs by nearly $20 million, restructured ADL's management consulting operations, and improved the company's profitability to the point where it now maintains a healthy backlog of sales. Ms. McNamara's areas of professional expertise include operations, product management and launches, supply chain management, and business process redesign.

During her tenure at ADL, she has served as head of ADL's North America Management Consulting operations and leader of ADL's Global Health Care Practice, where she managed large-scale projects for multi-national clients in the pharmaceutical and medical products industries. She has served on the firm's board of directors since 1998.

OVERLAP YOUR CIRCLES: MAXIMIZING THE THREE ELEMENTS OF THE STRATEGY CONSULTING BUSINESS

DR. CHUCK LUCIER

Booz·Allen & Hamilton

Chief Growth Officer, Senior Vice President

People, Passion, and Profits

The consulting business is, first and foremost, about helping people succeed – people inside client organizations, as well as people at your own firm. Intelligence, deep expertise, and analytical skills all matter, of course. But there's no shortage of smart, analytical experts across leading firms like Booz·Allen. A firm's success depends on the sincere desire of its consultants to help others succeed. Enjoying and enabling successes by other people has always distinguished truly great consultants.

Clients, of course, come first. Booz·Allen's market research confirms what any successful consultant knows: Senior executives select consultants whom they trust to work *with* them. Trust grows out of mutual success – collaborative efforts in which the consultant helps the client's organization repeatedly achieve significant performance improvements. With all the pressure on short-term performance, executives can't afford consultants who merely rubber-stamp their ideas. They need consultants who will listen to, understand, and empathize with their challenges; who will collaborate with them to develop and implement a successful answer. Successful consultants combine the ability to help the client organization win with a sincere interest in helping individuals within the organization succeed.

A consultant's best clients are always those people he or she has already helped succeed. By putting the client's needs first – those of the individual and the organization – the consultant ultimately becomes a trusted advisor. A client I've worked with occasionally during the past 15 years called recently and said, "I really need your help. We're considering a major acquisition that will make or break our business. Can you be involved personally? I trust you." It doesn't get better than that.

Helping people inside the firm matters too: The best colleagues, like the best consultants, are the people you have helped succeed. We (and other top management consulting firms) recruit truly amazing young people. The fun part is challenging people to stretch, to try to accomplish more than they think they can. In my own career, I know that I grow and learn every day. We try to stimulate rapid, continuous development in everyone at Booz·Allen. Of course, that requires time and commitment on the part of senior consultants. During the recruiting process, I make personal commitments to people we would like to hire. I promise that if they join Booz·Allen, I'll help them grow and have the most successful possible career – whether at Booz·Allen or elsewhere. Many of my colleagues at Booz·Allen – as well as many of my clients – are people to whom I have kept that commitment.

Consulting, especially strategy consulting, is an apprenticeship business: People learn consulting skills by observing great consultants and by assuming increasing levels of responsibility under the watchful eyes of experienced seniors. Helping others grow is not only fun, but it's enlightened self-interest. Altruism didn't motivate master craftsmen in medieval guilds to take on apprentices any more that it motivates me to recruit new associates. Consultants, like the master craftsmen of old, need apprentices to help get the work done. The more skilled an apprentice becomes, the more they can do, freeing up the "experienced master" to concentrate on the most demanding tasks. The more I can help my colleagues develop superior skills, the more I can concentrate on the activities that I do best, and the more our team will succeed.

Profession and Business

Make no mistake: The starting point may be helping people, but consulting is a business. Like any other business, we measure our success at the bottom line. Profits matter. As it turns out, helping people is good business.

Fifty years ago, Jim Allen, one of the founding partners of Booz·Allen & Hamilton, and Marvin Bower, the man who shaped McKinsey, engaged in a famous debate about the fundamental nature of consulting: a profession or a business? Bower, arguing the side of consulting as a profession, insisted that the consulting firm, like a successful law firm, should focus on doing the right things – for its clients, its people, and the development of ideas in its industry. If the firm fulfilled the obligations of the profession, the business would take care of itself. Allen took the opposite position: Consulting, he argued, is a business. Like any successful business – like our clients, Allen argued – consulting firms must offer attractive value propositions to all of their stakeholders. They deliver short-term performance while transforming themselves for long-term success.

Allen and Bower were both right. It doesn't matter where you start – a profession doing the right thing or a business offering attractive services – the answer is the same. One of the joys of consulting is that doing the right thing is always the right thing.

People matter. Profits matter. But a real understanding of the consulting industry requires the same discipline that strategy consultants bring to their client work.

The Structure of the Consulting Industry

The traditional segmentation of the consulting industry – strategy, operations, technology – never made sense. It confused our clients. It confused recruits. It confused consultants. As a strategist, I group large consulting firms into three segments, each with different economics based on different approaches to different sorts of problems: strategy firms, accounting consultancies, and what I call "application consultancies."

Strategy firms – McKinsey, Booz·Allen & Hamilton, Boston Consulting Group, and Bain – focus on developing unique answers to problems with the highest risk and the greatest long-term impact. Business unit strategy is the prototype. Sustained, superior profitability requires a strategy distinct from competitors, grounded in underlying economics and skillfully executed. Clients will pay premium prices to strategy consultancies that help craft and implement unique, competitively advantaged strategies. Of course, strategy consultants don't limit themselves to business unit strategy. We tackle other strategically important problems that require unique solutions – *e.g.,* organization, customer relationship management, and pricing strategies. Each of the large strategy firms derives the majority of its revenue from one or more of these other types of service offerings: McKinsey from overhead value analysis (overhead cost reduction), BCG from reengineering focused on winning through time-based-competition, and we at Booz·Allen, for supply-chain management and cross-functional solutions.

Strategy firms seek to work with the people inside organizations who make or support strategic decisions. A decade ago, this meant a fairly small group of people: the CEO, COO, business unit general managers (BUGMs), and strategic planners. Today, because intensifying competition and flatter organizations have pushed strategic decisions to a broader set of individuals within client organizations, we have the opportunity to work with a larger and more diverse set of people within any given organization.

The accounting consultancies – Accenture, Andersen, Deloite & Touche, and Price Waterhouse – use standard, repeatable approaches to help clients achieve operational improvements quickly, with minimal risk and at reasonable cost. Typically involving the selection and implementation of information technology, these kinds of operational improvements require some tailoring *(e.g.,* links to legacy systems), but focus primarily on delivering general capabilities, rather than unique solutions. The broader the scope of a given standard approach, the greater an accounting consultancy's revenues. In some cases, the majority of revenues for these types of firms accrue from a single business problem – such as Year 2000 *(i.e.,* computer programs unable to deal with dates after 1999) or the installation of enterprise resource planning systems, such as SAP or Baan. Outsourcing of corporate information technology departments or scale-intensive overhead functions has also been a major growth engine for these consultancies.

The economics of accounting consultancies depend on standardization. Whereas strategy consultancies have, on average, about eight staff per partner, accounting consultancies have about 35 staff per partner. The low leverage ratios of strategy firms enable senior staff and partners to stay intimately involved with the details of analysis and recommendations. In contrast, the high leverage of accounting consultancies defines their economic model: The only way to provide partners with the compensation they want, and clients with the prices they expect, is by generating fewer margin dollars across a much larger number of staff. In that environment, standardization is the only way to ensure quality.

Accounting consultancies target the CIO and other functional managers. Traditionally a very lucrative target, the CIO was the one functional executive who spent significant consulting dollars. As line managers have become more computer literate, CIOs are making fewer decisions about consultants, and the accounting consultancies are focusing more and more on business unit general managers.

The third segment, the ones I call applications specialists – AT Kearney/EDS, IBM, HP, Oracle, E&Y/Cap Gemini, SAS – are the consulting divisions of hardware and software companies. For these companies, consulting supports the base business: It creates demand for their hardware or software products, increases the value that customers receive from the hardware/software, accelerates customer use of the latest releases of the hardware or software, raises the customer's cost of switching to competitive hardware or software, and generates an additional revenue and profit stream. The typical consulting activities include selecting, installing, or applying the hardware or software – for example, SAS consultants helping a client's marketers use the software for data mining.

In addition to the three segments of "large" (more than $250 million in revenues) consultancies, a plethora of small niche players represents about half of the consulting industry's revenues. The majority of these "firms" are single individuals – consultants who have left large firms and are now on their own or retirees who are now consulting to their former employers. The remaining small players concentrate on one or two specialties, defined either by industry or by functional area. The principal advantages of these firms stem from their size: minimal overhead and the human scale where everyone knows everyone else.

Small firms suffer three significant disadvantages. First, they suffer from "feast or famine" cycles: Individual rainmakers tend to alternate between periods of intense selling and periods of doing the work. It's hard to maintain a balance of selling and doing. And it's hard to pay the bills when the rainmaker is in the selling phase of the cycle. In contrast, the many rainmakers at large firms move through different cycles, ensuring better use of all of the staff. Second, small firms can't help major corporations affect change globally, since they have neither the breadth of skills required nor the necessary geographic footprint. Since major corporations represent more than 75 percent of the consulting market, small firms can serve only a limited portion of the market. And third, small firms provide sub-optimal development opportunities for people: the chance to work extensively in one area, but not the opportunity to develop the broad skills that enable a person to become a general manager. As a consequence of these disadvantages, small consulting firms experience enormous turnover: One individual may consult for two or three years and then move on to something else; another individual decides to become an independent consultant.

The Evolution of the Consulting Industry

Three broad trends are reshaping the consulting industry: the growth of technology, changes in how we serve clients, and consolidation.

Technology, particularly information technology, has become pervasive in business. Information technology has either enabled or driven most companies' strategic priorities for the last 15-20 years. As a result, IT-related consulting has accounted for much of the consulting industry's growth. It's no surprise that applications specialists represented the fastest-growing segment during this period, followed by the accounting consultancies.

In the slower-growing strategy segment, each firm has taken a different approach to IT. Booz·Allen has created a strong information technology business linked to our strategy work: Information technology represents one-third of our revenues with commercial clients and an even larger proportion of our work with government clients. McKinsey has tried, unsuccessfully so far, to do the same. Since McKinsey's acquisition of a small IT firm (ICG) failed, they have gone back to trying to develop the skills organically. Bain accesses IT skills through a series of alliances called BainNet. BCG continues to eschew technology, remaining focused on strategy.

The second, less obvious, trend reshaping consulting is successive waves of change that have transformed the very nature of our work with clients. People usually talk about these waves in terms of new service offerings, such as business process reengineering (BPR) or e-business. But it's far more powerful to think in terms of changes in the nature of value-added by consultants, rather than in terms of new serviced offerings introduced. When I joined the industry in the 1980s, we provided clients with advice that we delivered in reports. While I'm proud that most of my clients implemented – or at least tried to implement – my recommendations, the industry-wide reality was that most recommendations weren't implemented. Advice, of course, still constitutes an important part of the consultant's value-added. But the center of mass of consulting activity has shifted in a fundamental way over time, toward more and more value-added. The next three paragraphs, while deliberately oversimplifying the industry, describe these changes.

During the late 1980s, consultants began including clients as integral members of the consulting team and embracing change management disciplines. Understanding and buy-in at client organizations increased. Clients genuinely tried to implement most of the industry's recommendations. But they still struggled with interpretation and implementation. For example, during the 1980s, a CEO who had been a client for many years said to me, "At the beginning of every month, I re-read the strategy you did for me three years ago. I think that I've finally figured out what you meant by this dot point." He pointed to a page in the report. "Am I right? Is that what you were saying?"

In the BPR wave, consultants began directly helping clients change the way they did business. We worked with clients to build capabilities – the knowledge, business processes, and supporting information technology required to deliver value to their customers. Clients benefited in two ways. First, by working together with the client to affect change, we closed the gap between interpretation and implementation. Second, shifting from giving clients answers to improving ongoing performance provided greater recurring benefits. It's analogous to the old Chinese proverb: "Give a man a fish, and you feed him for a day; teach him to fish, and you feed him for a lifetime."

In the most recent wave, e-business, consultants moved beyond capability-building and began partnering with clients to develop the business itself. Fees increasingly became a function of the client's results or an equity share in the venture. The dot-com crash brought this wave to a premature conclusion, contributing to the recent slowdown in the growth of the consulting industry in the United States.

The third trend changing the consulting industry is consolidation. From 1960 to 1995, the concentration ratio in the consulting industry didn't change: The proportion of the industry's revenue represented by the top five firms, the top ten firms, or the top 50 firms didn't change. During the past six years, however, the number of firms with revenues of $25 to $300 million has dropped significantly. Financial pressure and falling revenues are contributing to the decline of medium-sized consultancies. The collapse of e-business-oriented consultants, such as Scient and Viant, provides the most spectacular examples of the pressure on medium-sized firms. But a far more lasting trend is mergers of medium-sized firms that are extremely strong in one geography, industry, or service offering with larger consultancies. For example, two years ago, CARTA, one of the leading management consultancies in Scandinavia, merged with Booz·Allen. The merger has been extremely successful: CARTA retained their local client base, and together we've significantly increased our share of the global business of multinationals based in Scandinavia.

Pressure on medium-sized firms is, of course, a classic symptom of industry consolidation. However, broad consolidation in the consulting industry will be very slow because the mega-mergers that are the principal vehicle for rapid consolidation in other industries don't work in consulting. In my view, *no* merger of two major consulting firms has been successful in the long term. Mergers may succeed for a few years, while the principals of the acquired firm continue to drive the business; the acquiring firm typically insists on a three- to five-year earnout, ensuring that the principals are active initially. But once the earnout period is complete and the principals leave, the value of the acquired firm plummets. In a people business, what's the value of a firm without its best people?

The Future of Consulting

What is the future of consulting? Changing client demands are fueling a fundamental change in the consulting industry. Clients are demanding increasingly tangible and lasting results, fast – results that contribute to a company's competitive advantage. Today, customers, shareholders, and the best employees need and demand more rapid improvements in performance than organizations naturally produce on their own. For example, in the United States during the decade of the 1990s, the median "above average" performer among the S&P 500 sustained annual earnings growth of 19 percent and annual revenue growth of 12 percent – three times the growth rate of the global economy – while also addressing the greater expectations of workers and citizens. Increasing an organization's ability to change to meet the rising demands of all stakeholders is *the* challenge for leaders.

Consultants face the same challenge: We have to raise our game to help our clients raise their game. One client told us last year, "The old ways just don't work any more. We need ideas *and* actions. Paradoxical elements need to be synchronized and harmonized." Clients need clear solutions in our complex world; they no longer have the luxury of addressing issues sequentially – dealing with cost reduction during a recession, for example, and focusing on growth later. They need immediate performance that will yield lasting advantages.

The old paradigm – developing insight first, acting second – no longer makes sense. The most effective strategies evolve through a series of actions that create and exercise options; each major decision both stimulates new strategic insight and drives near-term actions. For example, understanding the possibilities and limitations of technology is crucial to the development of strategy; realizing the benefits of technology requires interrelated changes in strategy, organization, operations, and marketing.

The change in paradigm implies a redefinition of the consulting industry. Traditionally clients hired strategy consultants to create insight and accounting consultancies to help with actions. It was never an effective division of labor. Accounting consultancies implemented systems that created no business value; strategy consultants sometimes created recommendations without recognizing the difficulty of implementing them. Today, clients need consultants that truly *combine* strategy with technology and insight with action.

With the shift toward delivering more tangible value, pricing in the consulting industry is in the midst of irreversible change. Management consultancies traditionally charged fixed fees or weekly rates based on the number of expected hours a team would work. Increasingly, fees depend more on the value that clients receive – either because fees are explicitly tied to results or because the consultant has an equity share. Aligning client and consultant incentives is a win-win. Clients avoid paying big fees for unsuccessful consulting engagements; consultants who always deliver high-quality work earn more; consultants are motivated to accept engagements not only where they are confident of adding great value, but where they believe the client will be able to make the requisite changes and realize the benefits. Bain has been the industry leader in non-traditional pricing, starting with Bain Capital (an LBO fund) 20 years ago. Bain and Accenture are leading ongoing changes in the industry's fee structure.

For the past 40 years, consulting has been one of the most innovative industries—delivering both significantly greater benefits for clients per dollar of consulting spend (which has fueled double digit growth) and also increased compensation for consultants. The industry's future depends on continued rapid innovation. There's no doubt that significant innovation will occur. But which innovations will be most powerful and which consultancies will benefit the most are open questions.

The Consulting Culture

Consulting firms have remarkably different cultures – "remarkably" because we're all in the same business; we serve the same clients; and we hire from the same places. The differences are also remarkable because we all put clients first; we communicate in similar ways; and we perform similar analyses.

The biggest differences, of course, are between segments. Strategy firms organize and operate around their partners. "Know Who" institutions, strategy consultancies strive for two degrees of separation between people in the firm: Partners all know each other; each partner knows the eight staff nearby; anyone can reach for anyone. In contrast, accounting consultancies, given their focus on standardization, emphasize size, organization structure, and formal processes. The number of partners is much larger; partners can't all know each other; and most of the firms employ formal tiers, where some partners have more rights than others. Finally, the application consultancies are divisions of major corporations, significantly more hierarchical and process-disciplined than the strategy or accounting consultancies.

The differences in culture within each segment are nearly as great as those across segments. It's not a question of better or worse, right or wrong. The cultures are just different. For example, within the strategy consultancies, Bain in the early 1980s embraced a culture that said, "We are a team with a unique view of the world. We spend all of our time together socially. We buy all of our suits at the same place. We're very much alike, and that's a good thing because it lets us have the kind of impact that changes the world."

Booz·Allen is at the other extreme – far more heterogeneous than any other large firm, in any of the three segments. We have people who could fit at firms in each segment. As a result, we also have many people who wouldn't work at one of the other strategy consultancies. We embrace the diversity. The Booz·Allen culture says, "The great thing about this place is that we're all different. I love to work with all these people who know stuff that I don't know. The projects I learned the most on are the ones that are outside of my area. I can be a square peg in a round hole." Booz·Allen allows – actually requires – people to shape their own career paths and find mentors committed to their success.

To highlight a different dimension, some firms, like McKinsey, operate locally. Wherever possible, people are staffed on engagements near their home cities. People must be comfortable working on a variety of issues in multiple industries. They have the opportunity to work with the same people over and over again. In contrast, Booz·Allen operates transcontinentally *(i.e.,* across the U.S. or across Europe). The good news is that a person has a better chance of finding an opportunity that matches what she or he wants or needs to do. There are greater opportunities to specialize in an industry or functional area and to learn from a broad variety of people. The bad news is that travel is likely to be greater.

The Art of Consulting

The art of strategy consulting – I can't speak for the other segments – is expressed in developing workable recommendations, based on objective analysis, that help to stimulate beneficial change in the client organization. Where's the art in that statement? It's in weaving together three independent strands of activity – objective analysis, development of workable recommendations, and stimulating beneficial change in the client organization.

Twenty years ago, we did it sequentially: first, objective analysis; then, development of recommendations; and finally, managing change in the organization. Even then, the consultant's art was in thinking about all three strands in an integrated way. Although an engagement might start with a broad set of diagnostic analyses, consultants quickly have to narrow the analysis to the few issues that can make a material difference. What recommendations might evolve from each possible analysis? Which of the possible recommendations could be powerful enough to justify additional analysis? Are some of the recommendations theoretically interesting, but not really relevant for this client?

"Implementability" of the recommendations matters from the outset. Do key client executives share the view emerging from the analysis? Why not? Does the difference in view really affect the recommendations, or not? What other analysis can we do to demonstrate which view is right? What will be the obstacles to implementation? How can the recommendations be reshaped to increase the likelihood of successful implementation? Which clients might be "zealots" who will lead the implementation of the recommendations? What are their concerns?

Continually juggling analysis, recommendations, and change is a challenge at the best of times. But the real art of consulting is to bring the three strands together in the most difficult situations – in the situations where the consultant can add the most value. For example, we once did a strategy engagement for the head of one of General Electric's business units – someone who had been in the division for 20 years, who believed that the business was performing as well as it possibly could, but who had been required by the corporation to engage a consultant (not an atypical circumstance). Our analysis quickly pointed to a major improvement opportunity. But the business unit general manager refused to believe it. How could we help the business unit change in the face of adamant opposition from its general manager? In this case, we concentrated on what we believed was the one absolutely crucial analysis, refining and refining it until we (and the client's accounting department) were absolutely sure that it was accurate beyond any possible doubt. I spent 12 hours with that manager, one-on-one, working side-by-side at his conference table. We went through every number and answered every one of his questions. The analysis held up. Once convinced, the general manager proceeded to drive the rapid implementation of a broad change program that doubled the division's profit within 18 months. How did we know to focus quickly on just one analysis? How did we know which analysis? Why were we confident that by rolling up our sleeves and working through the analysis with the manager, he would change his mind? That's the art of consulting.

As a strategist, I often help companies change the rules of the game in their industry. It's exciting work; and seeing my clients change the world is personally rewarding. But this kind of work demands true artistry. Analysis looks backward, showing how the world has worked in the past. By combining analyses and creating powerful models, it's possible to understand the key levers that might change the rules of the game in the industry. But ultimately, no one can prove something that no one in an industry has done. Given the limits to analysis, how can we shape recommendations about what a client might do? How can we help the leaders in the client organization mobilize the company to try something that has never been done? That, too, is the art of consulting.

Should You Become a Consultant?

Should you become a consultant? Consulting is a weird business. Despite the industry's best efforts, none of us has been able to effectively communicate what it's really like to be a consultant. As a result, until you experience it, you can't really evaluate whether you'd be successful as a consultant.

Consulting firms, too, have only a limited ability to judge a potential consultant's long-term success. Even in strategy firms, only about 15 percent of the people we hire become partners (in accounting consultancies, the proportion is much lower). We hire only people who we believe have the potential to prosper in consulting. We make relatively few hiring mistakes; most of the people we hire are successful as associates. But over the next six or seven years, 85 percent of our people decide they would be more successful or happier if they pursue a different career.

With so much uncertainty, it doesn't make much sense for any individual to try to assess his or her long-term success in consulting. Sure, the pay is good, and the opportunities for growth, excellent. But the question for most people considering consulting ought to be, "Will becoming a consultant for the next three of four years maximize my career options and employability?" The value proposition of consulting to recruits has been and will continue to be that it is the fast track to corporate senior management.

The most successful managers, both in large corporations and in start-ups, are what we call zealots: capable of simultaneously delivering today's results, increasing the organization's competitive advantage tomorrow, and motivating people to fulfill the future vision. In the past, corporations defined distinct roles: manager, strategist, and change agent. With today's faster pace of change and greater demands for performance, the roles can't be separated. A leader has to continually trade off improved performance today with changes to improve for tomorrow; since measurement and reward can't evolve fast enough, people have to trust their leader to recognize and reward the new behaviors that are required. No company has enough zealots.

Consulting, especially strategy consulting, is a more attractive career than ever. It's the ideal place to learn the zealot's skills. Recent research on learning suggests that it takes about 3,000 hours of practice to become a gifted amateur; 10,000 hours to become a leading professional. Interestingly, the amount of practice required is similar for a wide variety of pursuits, including golf, music, and chess. My hypothesis is that about the same amount of practice is necessary to learn skills in business. In three years, a consultant can attain "gifted amateur" status in strategy and leadership – experience that it would take two or three times as long to acquire in a corporation. Admittedly, the managerial skills of P&L management don't develop much faster in a consulting firm than in a corporation. Since strategy consultancies are entrepreneurial, five years in a consultancy are sufficient to attain "gifted amateur" skills in management along with a "professional" level of skill in strategy and leadership – the world's best training for a zealot.

Lifestyle is the principal downside to a consulting career. Strategy consulting is unpredictable. We work on the most demanding, urgent problems – problems that clients often wait too long to address. It's not unusual for a CEO to call and ask for a meeting on Saturday or Sunday, or to ask a team to begin immediately. The good news is that the engagements that address the client's urgent, important issues are the most challenging and rewarding for the consultant. The bad news is that you never know when your client will call and need you immediately. Before I became a consultant, I was a college professor. As a professor, I was home with my kids every night; I coached Little League and soccer. As a consultant, I can't commit to coaching athletic teams; there's too much danger a client will call me away, and I won't be able to fulfill my responsibility.

We work hard to help people manage their lifestyle: We limit days away from home; an increasing proportion of our people work part-time (at all levels, including partner); we've created some career paths with more predictable hours and travel. But lifestyle continues to be one of the major reasons people leave consulting.

The Most Difficult Part of Consulting

At least for me, lifestyle isn't the most difficult part of consulting. Lifestyle is manageable: Draw and enforce lines; be home for birthdays and anniversaries; don't come back from vacation; when traveling to interesting places, take your family or significant other and stay over the weekend. In other words, find ways to make the consulting lifestyle work for you. Consulting provides a host of unique experiences – take advantage of them.

For me, the most difficult part of consulting is delivering tough messages to people in the firm. Since there isn't one standard career path at Booz·Allen, we have to provide very frank feedback about what's working and what isn't, so that people can chart the most productive course for themselves. Most feedback sessions are very positive: Honest, constructive feedback has enormous value to the person receiving it. Even when people are leaving Booz·Allen, our dialogues are almost always very positive. The vast majority of people who leave the firm make a natural transition from consulting to general management, either because of a great offer they can't refuse or because of a change in their desired work-life balance. That's a happy event for them and for us; alumni are among our best clients. But it isn't always easy.

The truly painful, but very important, aspect is helping someone understand they would be more successful in a career other than consulting. I learned the importance of this early in my career. One of our smartest recent hires just couldn't figure out the art of consulting. When I started to encourage him to look at some opportunities outside consulting, he pleaded, "Even if there's only a one-percent chance that I'll be successful at Booz·Allen, I want to continue to try." Although he made significant progress during the following year, it was painfully clear that he would be much more successful as a general manager – which turned out to be true. He has become an extremely successful manager in a high-tech business. However, because I didn't do a good job of counseling, this colleague suffered through an unnecessary year with us and delayed the start of his high-tech career.

The Best Advice for a Consultant

My best advice for someone in consulting is "overlap your circles." Circles? Think of the three elements of the strategy consulting business – clients, team, and intellectual capital – as circles. New consultants assume there is a trade-off among the three circles. After all, there are only 24 hours in the day, and if I spend them all developing clients, then I don't have time to develop ideas or a team. But that's wrong. Sure, in theory, a strategy firm could develop all three circles using differentiated roles. "You focus on people development; I'll bring in clients; and Susie will develop our best ideas." In practice, no strategy firm differentiates roles in this way. Every consultant needs clients; it's the essence of consulting. Every consultant needs ideas to find unique answers for our clients. And we all need to develop people as part of the large teams we deploy to tackle our clients' complex, multifaceted problems.

In strategy consulting, the same people are strongest in all three circles simultaneously. It's easy to think it's just a gift, but when we studied our most successful consultants, we found they behave in a different way than the people who are less successful. They overlap the circles. Each action they took simultaneously contributed to developing clients, ideas, and people. For them, there was no trade-off.

For example, most of the ideas we publish are stimulated by our client work. Often, we write articles with clients, deepening our relationships with them. Or we write with our teammates, helping develop their skills. Publications not only cause new clients to call us, but also stimulate the intellectual growth of our people. Offering juniors the chance to assume some of a senior's responsibilities simultaneously provides a development opportunity for the junior and frees the senior's time for client or idea development. While working at a client, each team educates the other teams about what they're doing. It's a great development opportunity for both the presenters and us in the audience. The discussion stimulates new ideas; because of their broader understanding of the client's challenges and agenda, each team is able to add more value to their engagement.

The same principle of overlapping circles also helps with work-life balance. For example, when my kids were in college, I led Booz·Allen's recruiting at my kids' schools. It was a win-win. The firm valued the time I spent at the universities, getting to know the faculty, making presentations, and meeting with students. But I also spent time with my kids. And when I went to the schools to visit my children, I also made the effort to meet with students or faculty.

Whenever I feel overwhelmed by all that has to be done, I look for ways to better overlap my circles.

Ideas and Knowledge

Throughout this chapter, I've focused on people, inside the firm and at clients. But strategy consulting is also about knowledge and ideas.

Ideas and knowledge are the raw material strategy consultants use to craft powerful, unique strategies for clients. Twenty years ago, Michael Porter argued that companies could pursue one of three generic strategies: low cost, product differentiation, or brand. But today, successful companies innovate – applying knowledge about technology or business models to craft and execute new-to-their-industry strategies. With knowledge increasing exponentially, the field for strategy today is far broader than Porter imagined.

That said, it's important to recognize that consultants are more like engineers than scientists. Scientists develop and test powerful new theories. In strategy consulting, that's a role academics or a handful of gurus try to play. Consultants, like engineers, try to make things work, using theory wherever possible, experimenting and creating their own rules of thumb where theory is inadequate. Our business is to help clients be successful. We use new theories created by academics and gurus where they're powerful; in the absence of theory, we develop rules of thumb based on our own experience or those of other consulting firms.

As the firm's Chief Knowledge Officer, as well as in my current role of Growth Officer, I'm responsible for Booz·Allen's creation and use of knowledge. We target several major studies each year: some descriptive, to understand what companies are doing or thinking; some large-scale efforts, to create and test new theories. However, those studies are only a small part of our knowledge activities. With the exception of a handful of Booz·Allen gurus, we systematically look outside our firm for new science – for powerful ideas we can apply. Internally, we focus on understanding our clients' changing needs; the new, powerful solutions we've developed at one client may be applicable to other clients (who aren't competitors); and the new adaptations of our methodologies and rules of thumb – literally hundreds of improvements and innovations each year.

"Knowledge" usually connotes explicit understandings. However, for strategy consultants, the most important knowledge is "who." Better than reading the latest theory is access to the person – whether inside or outside Booz·Allen – who can help adapt or apply the theory to a specific situation. Better than a statement of a methodology is the expert who can help adapt it to the client's issue. World class "engineers" – consultants with more than 10,000 hours of experience in a class of problems – are central to the competitive advantage of a strategy consulting firm. By ensuring that our best expert in an area addresses the most demanding problems, we simultaneously provide the best possible answer to our client's problem and enhance the expert's learning.

Even in ideas, strategy consulting is about people helping people.

Dr. Chuck Lucier is a senior vice president of Booz·Allen Hamilton, based in New York. He has been part of Booz·Allen for more than 19 years. In 2001, Dr. Lucier was selected by Consulting Magazine as one of the 25 Most Influential Consultants.

Dr. Lucier's client work focuses on corporate and business unit strategy issues for clients in a variety of industries. In addition to his client work, Dr. Lucier is Booz·Allen's chief growth officer, responsible for the firm's marketing and commercialization of intellectual capital. He is the author or co-author of a book and more than 25 articles, and appears frequently on speaking platforms.

Dr. Lucier has served in a variety of leadership positions at Booz·Allen, including the firm's first chief knowledge officer, leader of the Consumer Products & Retail practice, managing partner of the Cleveland office for eight years, and twice a member of the firm's board of directors. In 1995, Dr. Lucier launched the award-winning strategy+business magazine, the place to find the best ideas in business, which is sponsored by Booz·Allen.

Prior to joining Booz·Allen, Dr. Lucier was an assistant professor at the University of Iowa. He holds a BA from Wesleyan University, an MA and Ph.D. from the University of Rochester, and an SM in management from the Sloan School at MIT.

THE ART OF CONSULTING-
FIGURING OUT
HOW TO DO IT RIGHT

DIETMAR OSTERMANN

A.T. Kearney

Chief Executive Officer

Challenges for the Management Consulting Profession

As I think about the industry today, I think there are really two sets of challenges – enduring ones that have been part of management consulting since the profession's infancy, and then a new set created by the unprecedented amount of change that has washed over the business world in the last ten years.

On a day-to-day basis, I'd be hard pressed to name another profession as challenging as management consulting. You work with many different industries with varied challenges, and you're called upon to solve countless types of problems. Even if you have clients in the same industry – which would seemingly have the same problems – individual companies invariably are so different in their culture and organization that the process of solving their respective problems is entirely new. So there's no routine to follow.

A second continuing challenge for the profession is the issue of how to recruit, develop, and motivate talent. The only asset any management consulting firm possesses is the people who work there. So one of our chief priorities is attracting and retaining the very best people in the field. We're only as good as our ideas – and that means we need the smartest, most creative consultants out there.

As far as new challenges go, perhaps the first is the amount of specialization required. Years ago, management consulting was more like a general practitioner's medical practice. Each consultant dealt with a variety of clients when they were "hurting" and tried to apply some problem-solving to ease their troubles.

But that kind of generalist approach has become a thing of the past. The industry has become more mature, with more highly educated and specialized consultants. Today, consultants need deep industry expertise to even be asked to the table. In addition, they need specialized skills – such as expertise in IT or mergers and acquisitions, for example.

This maturing market brings its own set of challenges and opportunities. Geographically, industry maturation and market penetration varies widely. The United States, the United Kingdom, and Australia are probably the most saturated consulting markets today – in fact, there was little or no growth in the market in the United States in 2001.

But parts of Europe are a different story – particularly in Italy, France, and Spain, where as a percentage of GDP, management consulting is not as developed as in the United Kingdom or in the United States. Accordingly, those markets have been experiencing significant growth. For example, in 2000, we enjoyed a 56 percent growth rate in

Italy. This year in France, that number will probably be 25 percent to 30 percent.

But the biggest growth potential of all is in Asia. In my view, Japan, Korea, and China offer huge potential. Japan is the second largest industrial nation, but the resources they are investing in management consulting are still relatively insignificant. Now, though, with all the economic problems Japan is experiencing, the business community is opening up and beginning to take advice from outside management consultants – just as the American business community has for 50 years or more. That's translated into a 50 percent growth rate for us there.

Korea is a slightly different story. Unlike Japan, it has been an easier market for the global consulting firms – because it is the most Americanized of all the Asian nations. Traditional business structures in Korea (the conglomerate-style *chaebols*) are breaking up, and that creates significant restructuring issues. As a result, Korean businesses are hiring consultants left and right. In my opinion, Korea offers the most lucrative near-term opportunities for management consultants.

But China, of course, offers the biggest opportunity – not right away, but soon, perhaps five to ten years – because it is the world's most populous market. At A.T. Kearney, we're taking action now to seize that opportunity.

Today's Technology

Overshadowing all of these changes, of course, is the complexity of today's technology. Technology has become an integral part of any business. Indeed, it's inseparable from business, and it has added new layers of complexity for the consulting profession. Consultants constantly need to adjust how they go about solving problems.

And the very nature of the solutions we provide is changing, too. Technology consulting no longer forms some separate category – it has become embedded in every strategy or operational engagement we do. There isn't a business process that hasn't been touched by the Internet. Today, therefore, we cannot credibly provide a company strategic or operational consulting unless we understand what the Internet can do for that particular business. It's fundamental and critical.

In this regard, A.T. Kearney is well positioned with our parent company, EDS. That relationship gives us the capability to understand what the Internet is doing to business processes today. That's why I think the strategic alliance we made with EDS six years ago was a great thing for us. We now have EDS to help our people understand and deploy technology in a way we had not been able to do in the first 70 years of our existence.

Technology has become an integral part of any management consulting engagement. This is going to lead to an industry consolidation for the consulting profession. There is no future for management consulting without the ability to understand and implement technology. It has also been the major driver of growth in the industry. Supply-chain integration, online procurement, e-business strategy – these have formed huge markets in the last ten years, and we're seeing the next generation come along now.

The Internet was a wake up call. Every single process has changed, and we all must understand those changes or risk giving clients the wrong advice. The need for this understanding has become more dramatic over time.

Because of the ease with which information can be gathered through technology, clients themselves are becoming more experienced in the field of management consulting. They are learning how to measure results more accurately. I believe in the future, the fees for service arrangements will be changed to a success fee-based structure. We already see that today with contingency arrangements. That's another reason for consolidation – private partnerships cannot finance those arrangements.

The Art of Consulting – Techniques for Success

It is common in the industry to describe management consultants as merely problem solvers – a management consultant listens to the issues, finds the root causes of problems, analyzes them, and develops a solution. But that's not the full story.

Often companies don't hire management consultants simply to solve a problem, but to actually help implement the solution. In these engagements, people skills, project management skills, and a relentless drive to get the project implemented and finished become critical.

We also often have to help clients manage and succeed in turbulent markets. This process is much less mysterious than it might sound. There isn't an industry or a company that can't make money in any economic environment if they just do it right. Figuring out how to do it right is the art of what we do – why we're in the profession.

In the current downturn in the United States economy, we're all well advised to have adequate capacity or flexibility in the products and services we offer – consulting firms and their clients alike. Obviously, in growth situations you have to identify different parameters. We learn so much about so many industries in the good times, as well as the down times. As the economy gets better or worse, we learn as consultants to adapt to different situations, working side-by-side with our clients.

A.T. Kearney is extremely results-oriented and quality-focused. That's the essence of brand. A.T. Kearney stands for results – and for the quality of the consulting work. We want to be known in the executive circles, in the whole company, as consultants who brought tangible, bottom-line results – that we increased the economic value of a client company. If the assignment is growth-oriented, we want to show that we created new markets or increased share. If the assignment is focused on cost savings, then we want to show increased profits. If we're working on processes, we want our results to be measured by improvements in efficiency and productivity. That's a very hands-on, down-to-earth approach.

We also pride ourselves on having the broadest, most in-depth quality system in the consulting world. We recently gave it another boost by putting it on the Internet. Thanks to that, I have available to me at all times how we are doing on our quality commitments at the 300 largest accounts we are currently serving – based on input from the clients themselves. Every morning when I go to work, I check my dashboard to see what the status is – and take appropriate action. That's how we measure success.

Consulting Skills

You need a particular set of skills to be successful as a consultant. First, of course, you must be intellectually curious and sharp – otherwise, the problem-solving piece doesn't work very well. But while intellectual brilliance is a definite plus, you can't be too outspoken. It's a delicate balance you must achieve to sell your work.

You also need to be socially competent. This is a people business, and you have to sell and implement your own solutions and your own results, as well as your client's. You are constantly interacting with people on your team and the client's team. Knowing how to read people and get along with them is just as important as your intellectual capacity.

You must be able to move organizations to the next stage. You have to constantly be in contact with your team and with your client, convincing and persuading, influencing and questioning. The information you get back depends on the quality of the questions you ask.

You need to have a drive, a desire to succeed. You have to have speed and flexibility. Things change quickly; you must be able to respond accordingly.

It's also critical for us to populate our teams with experts who know how our client's particular industry operates, so we need people with deep domain knowledge. After we analyze a problem, we assemble people with the content expertise required to solve it. If it's a financial problem, we need someone with a background in finance. If the problem is in operations, we call on someone who has manufacturing or supply-chain knowledge. As a global organization, 62 percent of our business is outside the United States, and we always have local representation on our teams.

Our consultants are highly capable individuals who have both intellectual and social skills. They usually can grasp concepts quickly but also can walk around in an organization, making individuals feel comfortable and drawing them out, so they can understand the problem much better. It's not surprising that management consultants are drawn from the top MBA schools because our profession truly requires the best talent in the world.

Consultants are incredibly hard-working. We expect a lot of drive from the consultants we hire. They don't work an eight-hour day – they usually work 12- to 16-hour days. Our client's problems are critical and need to be fixed on a timely basis. Usually by the time the client has decided to use a consultant, they are behind schedule. I have always said we start the second shift when the clients go home.

An effective team is allowed access to information from all over the client company and can be trusted with it. Clients pay well for management consulting services. Since they expect a great deal in return, they usually realize that open access to information is necessary for their problems to be adequately addressed. Limiting access to information usually limits success.

In operating our business, we wouldn't be successful if at least 60 percent to 80 percent of our consultants weren't busy all the time. The number of people available for an engagement can be limited because, we hope, everyone is busy on assignment. But a client who has an urgent problem is not going to wait three months for us to be able to start an assignment. Most of the time they want to start yesterday.

The Consulting Lifestyle

The best advice I have received was from my father in-law, an accomplished football coach. He said, "Look behind you, and if there's no one there, chances are you're not a leader." I remember that every day.

That's the advice he gave me. The best advice I can give others is about balancing life and work. That's a critical issue that I don't foresee ever resolving itself. A good management consultant's time is constantly in demand. If you're working at the heart of a larger corporation's problems, you can't suddenly say, "I'm taking two weeks' vacation now. Call me in two weeks." In the meantime, the company runs into deep trouble. That's just not the way you go about it.

Again, a medical analogy: If a child is born at 4 a.m., and you're the obstetrician, you have to be there. If someone needs a major operation in an emergency, it needs to take place now, not two weeks from now. We are similarly bound in the management consulting profession.

When I started consulting 14 years ago, it was chic to be this hard-working person who had no private life. And then those consultants reached the age of 60 or so, and they called on their kids. And their kids would say, "Who are you? I don't have time for you. I'm meeting friends." Suddenly their children have grown, and these hard-working consultants are hurt. And they see what they've missed.

I like to believe it doesn't have to be that way. I am the father of four children – from two to eight years old. Just as you have to have time management skills in your professional life, you also have to have them in your private life. The important thing is not so much quantity but quality, and I believe that the smaller amount of time I spend with my family is more high-quality and intense than many other people spend in longer periods of time with their families.

You can't just assume you're going to be home every night at six. It just doesn't happen in this profession. But every weekend – unless our firm has a crisis – is entirely free for my family. My wife will likely disagree, but I adhere to that schedule 85 percent of the time. It's important to me.

A History of Leadership

I'm not sure I'm qualified to tell you the best way to reach the top of any business. Consultants are usually not necessarily the best managers because they're the ones who analyze problems and recommend solutions. But successfully running a company requires rigorous management style, execution, and follow-up. They are two different skill sets. There are only a few people who have both.

Few managers now have great intellectual, strategic-thinking and problem-solving capabilities. And few consultants have managerial talent. Usually the ones who happen to have both rise fast and achieve management positions. In my case, it was simple: I happened to be in the right place at the right time – three times. First, I became head of our German office; then, three years later, head of Europe; and one year after that, CEO.

I have great respect for my predecessor, Fred Steingraber, who grew the business from $30 million to $1.2 billion. He started this endeavor in 1983, when A.T. Kearney was a middle-level, Chicago-based manufacturing-consulting outfit. But Fred had a vision for the growth of the management consulting industry. Back then, we had $30 million in revenue, and Fred said we had to be a $1 billion firm by 2000. We achieved that vision in 1997.

It was a wild vision to grow a company that much in only 14 years. But supplying that kind of vision is what a CEO must do. During his leadership of A.T. Kearney, Fred stood for that vision, for that incredible growth. He also spearheaded the globalization of the firm – moving first into Europe, then into Japan, and then into the rest of Asia. Fred opened more offices than anyone else at A.T. Kearney.

The CEO and chairman of EDS, to whom I report, Dick Brown, has also shown incredible strength in managing EDS. That's what EDS needed two-and-a-half years ago, when he came in. The changes Dick has made in processes are rigorous.

Golden Rules for Clients and Consultants

I would say there are three golden rules for clients:

First, after a consultant is selected, it's critical to establish an open, trusting partnership. You each need room to breathe to be successful. If you micromanage the consultants because you are afraid that they might spend $750,000 instead of $600,000, then you are better advised not to hire consultants in the first place.

Second, there's no such thing as a consultant project. Every project should be shared. Consulting fails if it is not heavily supported – and, ideally, led – by a client team. Results are owned by the organization, and implementation becomes much easier.

Third, you need frequent and heavy interaction to keep the effort on the right track. The consultants drive the project and usually work with the best people in the client organization. Consultants have a tremendous amount of push. The client is advised to have daily or weekly interactions with their team to remain current and to make appropriate decisions if the consulting assignment takes an unanticipated turn.

For the consultant, I think there are two key pieces of advice:

First, be flexible and interested in constant challenge. If you like things set in stone, don't go into the profession. Wrong choice. You need to be someone seeking new challenges every day of your life. That's what this industry is about. But the rewards are tremendous.

Second, you have more fun in consulting if you consider it a long-term career instead of a stepping-stone for another career in industry. You need to have a bit of experience to be really good at this profession. You can hire the best MBAs possible, but it takes two to five years before they really understand industries, before they understand all the methodologies, and before they become really effective. This profession is much more rewarding if you're in it for the long run.

Dietmar Ostermann, 39, was appointed chief executive officer of A.T. Kearney, the management consulting subsidiary of EDS, in November 2000. He reports directly to EDS chairman and CEO Dick Brown. Mr. Ostermann is the fifth – and youngest – CEO and the first European to head A.T. Kearney in its 75-year history.

Mr. Ostermann was named managing director for A.T. Kearney's operations in Europe in May 2000. Previously, he served as A.T. Kearney unit head for Central Europe, responsible for operations in Austria, the Czech Republic,

Germany, Hungary, Poland, Russia, and Switzerland. Prior to that, he was managing director of A.T. Kearney in Germany and earlier served as New York-based leader for the firm's North American automotive industry practice.

Mr. Ostermann has served as client officer on several of A.T. Kearney's largest global automotive and manufacturing accounts. As a consultant, his specialties include manufacturing strategy, product development, corporate transformation, and efficiency improvement. As a unit head, he led A.T. Kearney to double-digit percentage growth in revenue, first in Germany and later in Central Europe.

Mr. Ostermann joined A.T. Kearney in 1989 and was elected an officer of the firm in 1995, following the acquisition of A.T. Kearney by EDS. Before joining A.T. Kearney, he was a manufacturing engineer for BMW and a plant analyst for Daimler-Benz. He has worked for A.T. Kearney offices in Düsseldorf, Prague, New York, and Southfield, Michigan, and served on client engagements throughout Europe and North America, as well as in China, Japan, Brazil, and Argentina.

A Hamburg native, Mr. Ostermann earned a BS in manufacturing engineering and an MBA from the University of Hamburg and an MS in industrial engineering from the University of Southern California.

THE DISCIPLINE OF CLIENT VALUE

LUTHER J. NUSSBAUM

First Consulting Group

Chairman and Chief Executive Officer

The Exciting Side of Consulting

As with most people who've been in business a while, my career has taken me through several business environments. I've been an executive with Cummins Engine, senior VP for marketing and operations with Businessland, and COO at Ashton-Tate, all great jobs, working with great people. But things changed in an important way when I took the job as CEO of Evernet Systems, a national systems integration company. It was at Evernet that I got into the IT services field, which became my door to consulting, a business that I love and that I find ideally suited to my abilities and temperament. I have a lot of energy, a lot of curiosity, and a high degree of self-discipline, a personality that the consulting field seems to particularly reward.

Several things get me excited about consulting. One is the diversity of assignments. It's never boring, never the same. You work with high-intellect people, so you're surrounded by people who challenge your thinking and your environment. I've encountered and worked with an immense variety of people, and we have learned from and taught each other. When smart, committed people challenge your thinking, you have to go through your logic very carefully, and you invariably wind up with a better answer. And, although this kind of supercharged environment can be pretty stressful, I can't think of a day that I've gone home without learning something new –

something that makes me think about things a little differently.

In the sort of consulting that we do at FCG, there is the potential for having a long-term impact, not just on individual clients, but on two important industries, healthcare and the life sciences. This is a major motivator for me, as it is for most of FCG's employees – we call them associates – because these industries deal with, literally, life-and-death issues. Healthcare in the United States has a lot of problems, and industry leaders are looking hard for ways to solve them. To be a part of these solutions is very energizing because there's strong, shared moral commitment.

From a pure business point of view, the competition is exciting. I'm a pretty aggressive competitor, and, as FCG has grown and moved into IT services, as well as consulting, we have begun to compete against the major players in the industry – Cap Gemini Ernst and Young, IBM, Accenture, CSC, and so on. To compete and win against companies of their stature is a real victory; I enjoy it and know our associates do, too.

In a sense, consulting is the ideal business relationship: We don't succeed unless our clients do. So much flows from this – the teamwork, the sense of a shared fate, the shared pride in accomplishments. You find out what's actually possible with your clients, your colleagues, and yourself.

The More Things Change . . .

Although business, like any other human activity, is progressive in the sense that each generation builds on the accomplishments of the last, this progress can be viewed, I believe, as the upward trend line of a series of cycles. This is certainly true in consulting, where the more things change, the more they remain the same. I've been in it too long to think things have really changed. You go through cycles and revolutions, and it's mainly the people who haven't been through the full set of cycles who think anything is new and unprecedented.

First Consulting Group is in information technology consulting and services, which has experienced a series of long waves over the last three or four decades. In each case, a new technology arrives and disrupts existing business patterns, which then resolve themselves into new patterns, in periods ranging from a year or two to decades. Depending on the technology, the effect can be deep or shallow – the mainframe computer, and then the personal computer, have wrought profound changes over the years; other technologies have had a more localized effect. Most recently, we've just gone through the first phase of the dot-com wave; as it has been absorbed by business, we have entered the consolidation period, when things slow down a bit, and are awaiting the next phase of the dot-com wave and the next technology in combination, which we believe will be the always-on, always-present network, driven by wireless and miniaturization.

At the same time, healthcare and life sciences are going through cycles of their own. Healthcare has had a very tough two or three years, but we're on the other side of that now. Healthcare is, so to speak, getting healthy, and part of that is that, for the first time, information technology is being absorbed quite deeply by an industry that has historically lagged behind other industries in the United States in that regard. Healthcare is responding to a combination of economic, scientific, and regulatory forces by adopting information technology and changed processes on a broader scale. We are, in effect, seeing the separate evolutionary cycles of technology and healthcare begin to converge, and I believe that the outcome will be major changes in the way care is delivered. Similar forces, though driven more by industry consolidation and new discoveries in basic science, are changing the life sciences industry.

To a great extent, IT consultants and service providers help clients deal with, and profit from, technology cycles by helping them understand these cycles. The objective is similar to that in military strategy – to keep them from refighting the last war. The PC wave, with its delivery of applications to the individual user, offered very different options from the mainframe wave, and the Internet and wireless will support radically new applications and offer still different options.

Selling and Delivering Value to Our Clients

At one level, the best definition of the value that leading consulting firms bring to their clients is the most common: getting results, because, ultimately, our clients aren't buying consulting hours or advice or reports or implementations. They're buying results, and we're there because the client is aware that, for any of a number of reasons, they can't get the results on their own. The buying decision for them is how they are most likely to get the results they want, which becomes a matter of evaluating how potential consultants work. For the consultant, in turn, the fundamental question is how to organize the firm and approach the work. We and our clients have the same goals; the issue for us is how to show prospective clients that we can achieve the goals and then get it done.

First and foremost for us, we concentrate specifically on two industries, healthcare and life sciences. While these industries have different business models – healthcare is primarily services, while life sciences is research, manufacturing, and distribution – the needs they serve are closely related, and we regard them as a single industry. Within this space, the FCG brand is very well known and understood. We have deep domain knowledge and very deep technology knowledge, so when we walk in, most people will have an awareness of the FCG brand, which helps enormously. We lay out the specifics we can deliver, depending on the kind of client – an academic medical center or a pharmaceutical company or a biotech company or a health-plan payer – as our initial way of engaging with the prospective client.

First, we want to be sure they understand the FCG brand; if not, we sell it. Our greatest strength in that regard is FCG's long track record of client satisfaction – we regularly score at the top in independent client satisfaction surveys. Beyond that, we want to confirm the FCG brand in their space, and then we want to deal with the qualifications we have or the kinds of projects we've done in their space; here we are able to cite some pretty impressive references, based on "exceeds expectations" performances and carefully nurtured through long-term client relationships. Then we explain the team we're going to bring to the client and the depth of knowledge and experience that team will bring. It's just a matter of presenting our unquestioned ability to achieve the results that the client is looking for.

Like many other aspects of consulting, our position is somewhat paradoxical: We bring deep knowledge of the client's business, problems, and objectives but, at the same time, an external, detached perspective. People want solid and empathetic knowledge of their circumstances, but an outside view, a perspective that is external to their business and suspends the conventional wisdom. If you're a client organization, and you talk to the same people day after day, you become convinced that you know what you're talking about, and you stop looking for new ideas. So you bring in consultants to provide an outside view and to challenge your thinking.

We bring knowledge of what's been done before, both successfully and unsuccessfully. We can bring five cases, for instance, that show that people have tried something that just doesn't work, even though it may sound conceptually neat. We bring detailed knowledge to systems implementations. There are usually three or four things about, say, configuring your software or setting up your internal processes that, if you'd known about them beforehand, you'd have done differently. We can bring that key knowledge.

We bring discipline. People often have a hard time accepting new ideas from people they work with closely or frequently. A consultant from the outside is seen, at least provisionally, as credible. In fact, one of the challenges for us is that when we get into really long-term engagements, we have to avoid becoming too closely identified with the client, which can cost us some of the "outside" aura.

We bring focused and applied research capability through our Emerging Practices group, based in Boston. We constantly look at the market and the technologies we work with and turn that knowledge into deeper insight and improved techniques.

We bring variable cost resources. People can gear up for a project without having to bring people onto their payroll and then having to lay them off after the project is over. They can just hire us to come in, get the results, send the bill, and go home. This not only avoids the obvious costs and disruptions associated with workforce churning, but it also avoids the hidden costs of having to bring people up to speed on a new project in a new environment. Although every project is a little different, we've done most of anything we work on before, so we're effective from the moment we hit the door.

Knowledge management is very important to us for several reasons. First, it allows us to reduce the cost of our services. We have developed a large base of standardized tools and techniques that we apply where a custom approach is not required or is not cost-effective for the client. These reside in KITE, our Knowledge-Information-

Technology Exchange. KITE is a huge, highly organized and accessible collection of electronic documents, tools, and techniques that "operationalizes" our approach to knowledge: Take from what has been done before, add value to it, and put it back for others to use. Our core knowledge base and our core set of methodologies, which we call First Steps, are the discipline structures we can take clients through and get much better results as a product of our experience. Since the contents of KITE are constantly circulating through projects, they are constantly being updated.

Standardized tools are, of course, not adequate for every phase of every project; in most projects, and in a nearly all large ones, there will be components that require some customization. Project plans have to be adapted to fit client capabilities; process designs have to reflect how the client wants to deliver care or do business. So, it's perhaps most useful to see standardized tools as literally that: We can help the client build a lot of different houses, but we don't re-invent the hammer for each job.

Good knowledge management also supports an important source of client value: knowledge transfer. Consultants are often accused of hoarding knowledge to make themselves indispensable and prolong engagements. This tactic is classic short-term thinking that results in a lot of resentment. Our approach is the opposite: We transfer knowledge to the client to ensure that the client is self-sustaining when we leave.

Each of these aspects of our practice is aimed at getting results, meeting – if possible, exceeding – client expectations, and leaving a satisfied client in the rear-view mirror.

The Ideal Client Relationship

The ideal client relationship is one that has developed over the long term and that is based on value delivered, candor, and trust. The first foundation of this relationship is the value that we add to the client – the results that we help the client achieve. Of course, to support the relationship, this value must be evident to the client, which is one of the reasons we must not only perform, but we must also communicate constantly: The client has to be aware of the value.

Candor is essential to all enduring client relationships. Good consultants offer it, and wise clients demand and respect it. It's easy, in the short term, to tell a client what you think the client wants to hear, but it's a tactic that defeats both sides. First, you may well be wrong; the client may have something very different in mind. Second, most clients can spot self-serving language from consultants very quickly; when they do, you've lost your credibility. Third, even if you get away with it, you will have cheated the client of one of the highest values a consultant can bring – honest and independent judgment. And, if the client is wrong, the consultant will have been an accomplice in failure. At FCG, we value candor so highly that our associates are formally evaluated on their willingness to say what they truly think, and no one is ever sanctioned for it – ever. The final decision, of course, is always the clients' and, naturally, we respect that, but we have an obligation to the client to help inform and guide that decision in the very best way we can.

Trust, as every consultant knows, is hard to win and easy to lose. Partly, it's a practical matter, a matter of confidence: Did we or did we not produce the results, enhance the client's value, as we were engaged to do? This is pretty much evident, and the trust extended to us as the work goes on is roughly proportional to how many of our promises we've been able to keep. But, partly, trust is an ethical matter: Do these consultants have my best interests as a client at heart, or are they merely here for the fees? This is where the client encounters not so much the consultants' practical ability as their culture. At FCG, we have developed a pretty rigid code of behavior: The client comes first. This is reflected in a lot of specific business practices. We will go the extra mile to meet the client's needs; if we make a mistake, we fix it, even if the client isn't aware of it. We staff and manage work according to the client's needs, not according to our revenue targets. This, obviously, can hurt us in the short run, but the short run isn't what we're interested in because we take a very long view of our business and of our client relationships. Ethical business isn't just right; it's good business, and it's the only business that's sustainable over the long term.

We like to stay with clients long-term for a couple of reasons. First, obviously, it reduces our cost of sales and administration. Second, it makes us more effective: The longer we have a relationship with a client, the better we understand their business and their culture. A good example is risk preference: Some clients are innovators and want to be on the leading edge; they believe pioneers get great land. Others believe pioneers get arrows; they want to see something that's been demonstrated at 15 other sites before they implement it. If you get a flavor of some of those client characteristics, you can do so much more for the client.

It's important to point out that a continuing relationship definitely does not imply non-stop consulting. We have clients to whom we have been close for years, but for whom we do only occasional work. For us, maintaining close relationships is a matter of continuing contact at multiple levels for whatever purposes are appropriate. For example, we helped create, and now participate in, the

Scottsdale Institute, a non-profit association of leading integrated-care delivery organizations. We work with the Institute on research projects, provide knowledge and expertise, and gain valuable market insights in return, as well as make FCG available for IT services and consulting work to the members.

Longer-term relationships also improve our effectiveness. On the first project we do for a client, we get to a level-one understanding relatively quickly: expressed needs, preferences, and so on. And, on that basis, we can typically bring a project off successfully. But it can take longer, especially with a major client or a highly complex organization, to gain the depth of understanding that will allow us to anticipate how the client will react, how the political chemistry of the organization will affect the long-term success of what we're doing, and so on. This is especially true with large-scale system implementations, hospital clinical transformation work – which is highly sensitive to physician and nursing attitudes – and extensive business process improvement work in HMOs and other insurers, where there are multiple business constituencies and stakeholders that have to be brought on board.

You have to get away from expecting idealized implementations. You're working in a real, human organization, with all sorts of politics and people and their intricate interrelations. You have to make sure your project socializes with that culture.

Facing Difficult Issues

Any project, no matter how well planned or managed, is going to run into an occasional snag. Certainly, good planning and management can reduce the likelihood and size of problems, but I've always placed a lot of importance on being ready for them when they happen. Some problems, such as staffing issues, delays, or disagreements, can be anticipated. Others, such as client business problems, unplanned project staff turnover, or third-party failures, often cannot.

The first key to heading off problems is to make sure you understand what it is the client really wants – not what the client *says* they want. Sometimes they're not the same things, and some careful probing – we're back now to candor and independent perspective – will uncover the difference. Getting this right is necessary for setting expectations with the client, which is a critical part of every project, without exception. Setting and managing expectations doesn't begin with project planning, of course – it begins with the sales call. Client success is about their relationship to expectations, and I believe that more consultants and more projects are undone by creating unrealistic expectations at this point than by almost any other mistake. The urge to over-promise to get the job and then figure out how to do it later is strong, especially with smaller firms, but it's almost invariably suicidal. Our approach at FCG is just the opposite: We under-promise and over-deliver. Moreover, we manage expectations throughout the project, not just at the beginning.

Managing expectations is really part of another firm principle of mine: Communicate, communicate, and communicate. You simply can't over-communicate. If there's bad news, you're a lot safer telling the client about it than hiding it and praying for a miracle. Three months into a one-year project, if we see the project is not going to be completed at the end of the year, and we tell the client it's going to take 15 months instead of 12, the client says, "OK, I understand." But they're not very happy if you wait until the 11th month to tell them you're going to tack on another three months. They conclude you're not in control and have not been doing a good job. This, by the way, is a rule that applies internally on the project team, as well: A good project manager wants to hear bad news when there's still time to do something about the problem, not when all the options have run out.

Another problem that can be anticipated is staffing conflicts and turnover. There are several kinds of these. In some cases, the chemistry may not be right; when that happens, we simply swap the consultant out. In other cases, consulting firms, ours included, are tempted from time to time to pull a person off a project because there's another one where that person is really needed. But you need to maintain the resources and the sense of continuity with a client, with a project, and with the project plan.

After that, it's a matter of formulating the right project plan. Plans that require too many innovations can pose problems. You'll have to try to manage through those issues and, as always, set appropriate expectations. Every successful project plan includes foresight for contingencies, "the unexpected." It's impossible, of course, to list all the things that can go wrong, but I plan along two dimensions – likelihood and severity. Some problems, such as illness on the project team, are likely, but not very severe because they can be managed through. Others are severe, but not very likely, such as a major business disruption or business failure at the client. The unlikely, low-severity contingencies get some attention; the likely, high-severity ones, such as vendor software delivered late or full of bugs, get a lot of attention. If there are more project risks than it appears we can manage along with the client, it's probably a good idea to redesign, delay, or even cancel the project. A delayed or cancelled project can usually be revived; a failed one usually can't.

Measuring Success for Our Clients

Client success can be measured in different ways, depending on what our clients want from projects and from us. But fundamentally, what we want is client satisfaction, and we'll go a long way to achieve it. Regardless of what their expectations were, we want people to say that we met them. The closer we get to a result that is related to the top five factors our client believes are strategic to their success – not tactical – the better we like it. We know then we're going to have more meaningful impact.

If our clients perform better in their marketplaces than our non-clients, that's the ultimate measure of success from our perspective.

Determining FCG's Direction

Creating a vision for your organization and deciding its direction are not terribly complex. You talk to a lot of people. You get the conventional wisdom. And then you ignore it. By the time it's conventional wisdom, and everybody understands it, it's too far into the trend to be meaningful to you anymore. I read a lot and look for opportunities. We're looking for high-impact undertakings; if we can do a few things that are really significant and meaningful, I believe we'll make our way very well.

Setting direction is a matter of integrating two tactics into a single strategy. These are, first, following the market and, second, leading it.

We're 21 years old now. We started out doing IT strategy work for clients, sitting down with them and looking over their next three to five years to see what systems they needed. That led us to get into selection. We once said, "You need a patient accounting system," and the clients responded, "Well, what patient accounting system?" So we helped make the selection. Then the clients said, "Will you help us write the contract?" And when we did that, they said, "Can you help us implement it?" Some of what you do just evolves from your relationship with the clients – it's just a natural migration.

A year-and-a-half or two years ago, we got into outsourcing – the other side of things – because our clients said, "Can you help us run what you've helped us assemble here?" We got into infrastructure work because when we did implementations, we broke the infrastructure. So we just keep going and migrating and moving and evolving.

This progression was reinforced by our learning early on that clients tend to prefer consultants who can take them through the entire systems cycle, from planning to selection, implementation, management, and operation, and we've extended our capabilities along that cycle as we've identified opportunities and built the firm. But the lesson is clear: Let client needs guide you so you don't get too far ahead of the market by offering services no one wants – at least not yet.

At the same time, however, consultants are expected to be leaders, and we have tried to identify those areas where new technology and new applications offer a real promise for substantial improvements in our clients' operations. Of course, this is easier with some technologies and market segments than others. Hospitals, for example, are culturally conservative and risk-averse and have historically been skeptical about getting very far out on the technology curve. Physicians are a tough sell if they don't see clear and immediate value for their patients and practices. Our approach has been to create market hypotheses and test them constantly against reality, while trying to shape reality just a bit by working for industry segment leaders, the "early adopters," where new ideas and technologies that can get a hearing have the best chance of success.

Of course, we have occasionally backed the wrong horse – being wrong once in a while is the price of trying to stay in front. We thought the computer-based patient record would penetrate healthcare much more rapidly than it has, for example, and that computer-based physician order entry would catch on as soon as it got easier to use; in fact, it's turned out that adoption of these applications is being driven much more by regulatory and quality-of-care concerns than by the applications' intrinsic appeal.

The lesson, to me, is clear: Part of leadership is being willing to take sensible risks. And FCG has always sought, and will always seek, the leadership position.

Strategic Risks Worth Taking

Risk is part of any business venture, and it's a factor in every strategic decision. Risk-taking is not gambling; it's the careful calculation of potential for gain and loss, made with as much information as it's practical to get. Note that I didn't say "possible" to get; very few risks can be allayed with the information available within the time horizon for the decision. At some point, I've found, I have to accept the residual risk or resign the game.

Part of FCG's growth and evolution has been learning how to take risks in the context of the services we offer and markets we serve, and which ones to take. For us, since high risk and high reward tend to go together, it's a matter of taking higher risks for greater rewards.

Historically, our biggest disappointments have been taking significant risks to do things that had a very small impact on our clients or on the firm. We have built and launched new services, for example, only to find that there was less demand than we thought there would be, or that they did not accomplish for the client what we expected them to. Sometimes we were guilty of not having read the market or our own capabilities clearly enough; in other cases, the market changed or other events intervened. The latter is, of course, "pure" risk – the consequences of things that we could not reasonably have foreseen.

There are two "faces" of strategic risk decisions. The first is how likely a given risk is and how grave the potential consequences; the second is what you do if things go the wrong way. Unlike the old joke about doctors – that they can bury their mistakes – consultants, like other business people, have to live with theirs: disappointment, financial loss, and painful staff reductions. We're continuously trying to define our practice around big-risk, big-reward; small-risk, small-reward. We try to make sure that, in our portfolio, the risks are digestible with where we are financially and where the business cycle is. We're still trying to dramatically improve our performance in assessing risk.

At the same time, though, while there are many things you want to avoid, if you start trying to play defensive, then you're not very effective. The history of American business is littered with the failures of companies that developed a fatal resistance to risk. We're oriented to walk into the client's office with a list of what we want to do, what we want to accomplish. We try not to think of the negative – the things we ought to avoid. It's like standing on the tee with water in front of you and saying, "I don't want to hit it in the water!" And the last thought you have is exactly where the ball goes. We just really avoid thinking in those terms.

One area in which we are calculating risk carefully is in extending our services into non-health-related markets, such as financial services, manufacturing, and distribution. We've learned from past forays – for example, into healthcare delivery consulting in Europe, where we lost a lot of money on what seemed like a good idea – that it's too risky to build a large and expensive delivery capability in advance of knowing whether we can serve a new market effectively. What makes more sense, we think, is to undertake small, carefully defined projects in a new market, subject them to rigorous evaluation as we go, and avoid making major resource commitments until we're sure that this is a market we belong in.

On the other hand, one risk we'll take when we identify a solid opportunity in a fast-evolving new market is an acquisition. The logic here is simple. Since it can take several years to do a good job of building a new, specialized practice from scratch, the only practical way to field a good team fast is to buy one. This is what we did when we at FCG grasped the extent to which healthcare was becoming drug-based and, as a result, acquired Integrated Systems Consulting Group in 1998. ISCG was a first-rate technical services firm with a large pharmaceutical and life sciences client base and an entrepreneurial, informal culture like FCG's. It was our first acquisition after going public, and it almost doubled FCG in size overnight. Although it took a little time to work out the organization, it has been a great success.

Managing in a Turbulent Market

The consulting market can be quite turbulent. Notoriously, even modest economic downturns in markets we serve can result in much deeper downturns in consulting. Clients stretch out projects, downsize them, or eliminate them altogether. Reduced revenues intensify competition and, by constraining salaries and benefits, make it harder to retain good people. Although the pharmaceutical and life sciences market, which is about 40 percent of our business, is pretty profitable and stable, healthcare works with much smaller operating margins and has gone though several tough years as government and employers struggle to hold down healthcare expenditures.

We're a public firm, so we have a fiduciary responsibility to shareholders, in addition to our associates and to our clients. Our way of managing in turbulent times is to "tier" our response with a three-level hierarchy. Level 1, at the bottom, is cash-oriented; Level 2 is profitability-oriented; Level 3 is growth- and profitability-oriented.

When you go from an up cycle into turbulent times, and revenues fall, you drop down in the hierarchy. You begin to focus on profitability, or you might have to drop further down to focus on cash preservation. You have to get the resources aligned with the demand, spend more energy on collecting receivables, and delay all but absolutely essential capital spending, so you can manage your cash flow through the down cycle. But as the market turns up again, you have to be adept enough to stop dwelling on the things that helped you preserve your space through, say, a six-month or nine-month period. Now, on the other side, you have to become expansionist, to build staff and capabilities, to begin taking risks again, and to figure out how your business is going to grow profitably.

It's important to communicate your actions to everyone in the firm. When we've had to cut discretionary expenses or reduce staff, we've been honest about it. If you try to hide the pain, your people find out anyway, and you lose their trust. You manage through the turbulent times and communicate to your organization that you're in a tight cash-flow condition now, and here are all the appropriate things to do. Then when you're in a time of growth-and-profitability, there are other appropriate things to do. Your associates need to understand you're not just running from one side of the boat to the other; what you're doing is an inevitable response to a cycle through turbulent times.

This is, essentially, what FCG has done over the last couple of years, as the healthcare industry went though a period of severe revenue constraints and rising costs, and that side of our business got hit pretty hard. We had to take some fairly stringent measures to manage cash, including pruning low-demand services and laying off some people – something we go to great lengths to avoid. None of it was fun, but it was necessary to preserve the base that we're now expanding from again.

The important thing is to recognize when you have to "downshift," so to speak, and do it promptly. Delaying and hoping for the best, which is the most common response – and one with which I can humanly sympathize – only compounds the problem. What might have been minimal downsizing and reductions through attrition winds up being massive layoffs that not only hurt those who are laid off but also leave morale and productivity problems in their wake and leave investors dubious about your credibility.

Finding Opportunities in Turbulent Markets

In turbulent times, consulting firms have revenue problems because their clients are having revenue problems. The clients think they can't afford the consultants and either fire them or don't hire them. The odd thing is that they're often wrong. Consultants are a good investment whenever an organization has to confront change; in good times the change is welcome by the client, and in bad times it's not, but it happens anyway. A good consulting firm develops the skills and industry perspective to help the client manage under either scenario.

In difficult times, cost is always the common denominator. If times are difficult, and you're going toward cash, then your clients are probably going toward cash, as well, and cutting expenses. So you can provide services that meld immediately with what they're doing. They might have been focused on their growth and profitability six months ago, but now they're saying the only projects they'll consider are those that will help reduce their costs or improve their cash flow. If you can respond to those immediate needs, you'll be in great shape.

With acquisitions, the old saying applies: "The time to raise money is when you don't need it." If you were able to put together a war chest during the up cycle, you can buy companies during the down cycle because they're far less expensive then. If you don't have a treasure chest of cash, your currency, your stock price, has now dropped, so the acquisition isn't any less expensive than it was before, and your shareholders are not amenable to your paying very high dollar amounts when they think the share price is depressed. No matter what the exchange rate between the two companies is or how attractive it might look conceptually, acquisitions are really hard to sell, so to speak, at that time.

Being Successful as a Consultant at FCG

FCG is a goal-driven company at every level. Every activity in the firm is directed to specific objectives and reviewed periodically for effectiveness. If it isn't hitting its objectives, we change the process or reconsider the goals. At the same time, we have a highly collegial, team-oriented culture, where virtually everything of importance is accomplished through groups whose leadership identifies objectives and manages towards them. The ability to work successfully in this environment is a key factor in recruiting.

Relative to setting goals for individuals, at FCG each person is typically a member of several different teams. At any point, you might be a member of your client team, your practice team, and your business unit team; and then you might be on a task force relative to changing something within the firm. Each of those teams has a set of goals, so we want individual contributions to the team, and we want a report of the progress of the individual and a report of the progress of the team. It's highly complex in terms of what we're envisioning and the measurement systems that are required, but we've managed to build it as a set of routines and systems, and it works pretty well.

We have about 2,000 people in the firm. Our fundamental belief is that, if we can describe easily, carefully, and concisely to people what we want, we'll get 50 percent better performance than if we leave it fuzzy, ill-defined, and unclear. So goals are extremely important. Getting clear goals at the individual level, linking them to the goals of the various teams of which the individual is a part, and then linking the goals of all those teams to the purpose of the firm – all that is complex but critical.

Shortly after joining FCG, I got involved in a human resources task force, co-leading it with an individual who'd been around a while. We redesigned the whole professional compensation and development system for the firm, articulating what we wanted in consulting. We set up six "silos." Each of these is a set of skills or abilities on which every associate is formally evaluated every year:

Foundation skills: You must be able to write well, speak well, and handle complex meetings dealing with conflicts and all sorts of issues.

Technical skills: Some of these can involve industry domain knowledge, and some can be technology; often it's a combination.

Practice and relationship development skills: Consulting ultimately revolves around being able to sell yourself, your team, and teams of other people to your clients.

Project management skills: You have to be able to manage projects in an extremely disciplined way.

Leadership abilities: We need this leverage to drive the business.

Decision-making ability: Some people can see ten facts and make one type of decision; another will see the same ten facts and make a much higher-quality decision. This doesn't seem to be very teachable; it seems to be innate. Some people are just better at making higher-quality decisions than others, given the same set of facts.

These "silos" are complemented by a set of core values on which we also evaluate our associates. These include accountability, integrity, commitment to quality, achievement orientation, adaptability – all things we work to embed in the firm's culture by hiring and promoting in accordance with them.

Successful Teamwork and Team Leadership

For successful teamwork at FCG, all those skills come together – not just the technical skills, but also the ability to perceive and read people well, the ability to communicate effectively, ask better questions than somebody else does, and probe more deeply to understand more about how the client's business is put together, so that the project can be successful in meeting their needs. So for a team, you're looking for technical skills, a variety of intangible skills, and then team leadership to pull all those disparate people together.

Consultants, by their very nature, have strong egos, a strong sense of presence, and strong views, and you need very good leadership to make sure every one is heard – to call them out, to get all the alternatives voiced and understood – but then to be decisive about setting direction and leading the consultants to make it happen.

A great leader exudes discipline, discipline, discipline. When you're responsible for delivering a project, you have to set up some level of command-and-control, so you can really get the discipline established that will carry your project through. Creativity is often needed in the early part of the project, but once you establish what you're trying to accomplish on deadlines, great leaders really have to get down to the disciplined, command-and-control structure to deliver the final result.

Leading a consulting firm is like leading a group of lawyers or an educational institution. You have a set of organizational goals that are inherently very complex and require a high level of communication and collaboration. You also have a group of highly energized, very independent, extremely talented people, and in leading those people, you have to give them purpose beyond their individual accomplishments. It's important at FCG to have a high purpose, something that's noble and achievable that is beyond what the individuals could accomplish doing consulting on their own. That's partly about establishing the FCG brand, but it's ultimately about having an impact on the industry we serve.

To keep my edge as a leader, I'm perceptive, and I have good instincts. I think you have to be that way to be able to head up a modern consulting organization like this one. You have to be intuitive: If you see 1 + 1, you have to be able to leap to at least 4 or 5 and see the trends, see what's moving. You can't rely too much on what's written. I get frustrated when people ask me about something that has been written; by that time, it's usually too late even to respond. You have to find out what they're *not* saying and where the gaps are and sometimes what clients haven't even recognized. You can't *talk* to them and see what's happening; you just see the trend and *know* what's happening ahead of time.

A Look Ahead at Healthcare and the Life Sciences

In many ways, American healthcare is superb. Our physicians are probably the world's best diagnosticians, and we lead the world in medical technologies and innovative pharmaceuticals. If you get sick in America and have either good private insurance or some form of government coverage, you'll get generally good care delivered by excellent, dedicated people. But the healthcare industry in the United States is recovering from a period of fairly serious revenue and cost pressures and is facing other difficulties.

American healthcare has a number of fairly serious long-term problems. We provide healthcare not through a nationally uniform system of insurance, but through a patchwork of government programs and employer-funded coverage. This leaves a lot of the population vulnerable, when people are self-employed or when employers are forced to reduce benefits in the face of rising costs. The result is that we have around 45 million Americans with no health insurance, leaving most without a reliable source of medical care. At the same time, our costs are rising steadily, driven largely by the growing reliance on increasingly sophisticated drugs that turn acute diseases into chronic ones, which extends life spans but increases overall healthcare consumption. The two effects – more expensive drugs and longer-term usage – have a compound effect on costs, which threatens to push more people out of employer-based coverage, especially as we move into a period of slower economic growth.

Our healthcare also has had some fairly serious quality problems, which have been documented by the Institute of Medicine. These are largely the result of the fragmentation of care delivery in the United States and our slowness in implementing the information technologies that can prevent the kind of errors that occur in such an incredibly complex, information-saturated environment. The information technology problem is being addressed, both by the initiatives of individual insurers and care delivery organizations and by employer initiatives such as the Leapfrog Group. The fragmentation problem has much deeper structural roots and, although information technology can help provide some degree of clinical integration, it cannot solve the underlying structural problems. This is true, as well, of the Internet: Although the Internet can be of immense help in changing some business processes, empowering consumers and supporting some kinds of clinical information management, it can't overcome the fundamental weaknesses in our healthcare system that have their roots in national policy decisions or economic forces.

It's becoming clear that our current approach to healthcare will have to change over the long term. What will replace it will probably be the sort of thing Americans prefer, a mixture of private and government initiatives, but with a larger government component, including, I believe, some form of universal insurance coverage, again probably combining private and government funding. Consumer influence in healthcare will grow steadily.

The pharmaceutical and life sciences industries, I believe, are in their Golden Age, with discoveries in the basic sciences, in genetics and biochemistry, occurring almost faster than they can be assimilated and applied. The drug companies are encountering some consolidation pressures, and legislative restrictions are being applied to some research directions – note the recent controversy over stem cell research – but I think there are many directions for success. For example, "personal medicines," based on individuals' genetically programmed responses to drugs, will allow us to eliminate the trial-and-error prescribing that we've been forced to do until now and will aim the drug exactly at the disease. The pharmaceutical industry has absolutely transformed healthcare in my lifetime alone, and I expect the transformations to continue.

A Look Ahead for the Consulting Industry

I think where the consulting industry is sitting now is similar to where we were around 1990 and 1991. Consulting took a pause and went backward a little. We were between waves then, as we are now – from late 2000, through 2001, and carrying over a little into 2002. But I see another really strong period from 2002 or 2003, through 2010. I think that as our society and business institutions become exponentially more complex, fluid, and based on technology, the consultant's stock in trade – the ability to apply highly specialized knowledge and skills combined with an independent perspective, for exactly as long as it's needed – has become so central to the world that continues to evolve, that consulting is going to have its own golden period again.

As far as developing hotbeds around technology are concerned, I think it's back to the waves. I think there will be major new areas that will continuously open up. I know people are enamored with wireless now. Wireless is a technology – it's not really a movement, not an application. We're much better off when we can ride the big waves of application, such as CRM or ERP or process re-engineering or the dot-coms. Fully integrated systems and major implementations tend to drive the market pretty strongly. New technologies and their implementation, though still important, tend to drive the market in a less significant way.

There have been massive waves of things that make people want to try to understand what other people are doing in common and then take them into their businesses. When those waves happen, consulting is at its peak. When we're between those waves, and we just have the normal sharing of best practices, some innovations, and specialty knowledge, we experience a pause – it's not a white-hot area. But you just go through waves. I think there will be another white-hot wave – we just don't know when.

Best Advice

The best advice I ever got was from the school of hard knocks – I've learned far more from my mistakes than I've ever learned from somebody's advice or counsel. You can't really learn about something till you've experienced it. Then you understand truly the implications of making bad decisions.

My daughter's long recovery from a near-fatal automobile accident several years ago changed my life dramatically. People comment now that I probably handle bad news as well as anybody else. It took an awful lot of bad news for me to learn you don't have to get uptight. You just listen to the news and figure out what to do.

My daughter and I were sitting, talking, not long ago, and she said she'd like to go back in time, if she could, in Michael J. Fox's DeLorean from *Back to the Future,* to the scene of her accident – and let it happen – because so much positive has happened out of the accident. She found her husband; the family has really pulled together; I've changed and mellowed; there's just so much good that came of it. It dramatically turned me around.

Applying the personal to the business, I can now say that what is, is. Now let's go figure out how to make something positive out of it.

The Golden Rules of Consulting

There are only a couple of fundamental rules. First, be empathetic with the client; put yourself in the client's shoes. Then take yourself out of those shoes and apply a broad enough perspective to see the client outside of how the client sees himself or herself.

If you can't be "schizophrenic" and see things both ways, you won't be successful. If you see things only in the consultant's broad perspective of what the client "ought" to do, you won't understand enough about why they are who they are, so you can help them change. I've often said that it's only by understanding why they are the way they are that you earn the right to recommend that they change. That's probably the most important rule that will serve a consultant.

Luther J. Nussbaum is chairman and chief executive officer, providing leadership to First Consulting Group. FCG, a 2,000-member, $240 million public consulting firm, is the leading provider of consulting, systems integration, and outsourcing to the healthcare, pharmaceutical, and life sciences industries.

Mr. Nussbaum is a 17-year veteran of the computer industry, having served most recently as president and chief executive officer of Evernet Systems, Inc., a national network systems integration company. Mr. Nussbaum was twice named to Computer Reseller News "Top 25 Executives" in the computer industry.

Prior to Evernet, Mr. Nussbaum was the president and chief operating officer of Ashton Tate, a microcomputer software development company. He entered the computer industry as senior vice president of marketing and operations of Businessland, Inc., a worldwide reseller of personal computer products and services, after more than a decade in senior management at Cummins Engine Company.

Mr. Nussbaum received his BA from Rhodes College and his MBA from Stanford University. He serves on the boards of Emergent Information Technologies and two private entrepreneurial companies, the Olson Company and Command Packaging.

GIVING CLIENTS MORE THAN THEY EXPECT

BRADLEY M. SMITH

Milliman USA

Chairman

The Question All Clients Ask

Conceptually, consulting is a pretty simple business. I believe all clients ask one question. Contrary to popular belief, it is not, "How much is it going to cost?" or "When is the project going to be completed?" although many clients do ask those questions. The question all clients ask is, "What do you think?" "What do you think the reserve should be?" "What do you think the premium rate should be?" "What do you think the pension liability is?" It all comes down to the question, "What do you think?"

There are many implications to that question with respect to being a successful consultant. One implication of the question "What do you think?" is that you have to be an expert in something. You have to be an expert in a continually changing environment.

The object of the question changes over time. This creates many challenges for the consultant, but it also makes consulting very rewarding. It is exciting to know that, as the world changes over the course of a career, there will always be a need for consultants who can think through solutions to difficult questions. I believe the consulting business is changing at a much faster pace than ten or 20 years ago, when the subject of the question "What do you think?" would stay the same for a longer period of time than it does today. Now, the subject of the question changes constantly. This is one reason that consulting is more challenging, as well as more rewarding, than it was in the past.

Six months to two years from now, clients are not going to be asking you the same questions they ask today. While solving the problems of today, consultants have to simultaneously reinvest in their knowledge base to prepare to answer the questions clients will be asking tomorrow. As a consultant, you have to continually reinvest in your knowledge and experience base to keep these amortizing assets whole.

The second ramification to the question "What do you think?" is that clients have to care what you think. As a consultant you must be an expert in a given topic, and your clientele, and potential clientele, have to know you're an expert. Some consultants are very insular and inward-thinking. They are constantly replenishing their knowledge base, but they are not communicating to anyone that they are an expert in a given topic or area. If you want to be a successful consultant, you have to be an expert in a given set of topics, and your potential clientele need to be aware of your expertise. Therefore, your responsibility as a consultant is three-pronged:

1) You have to complete your current assignments to the satisfaction of your clients.

2)   You have to reinvest in your constantly amortizing knowledge and experience base.

3)   You have to communicate to your clients that you are an expert in the ever changing environment in which you consult.

In short, you have to constantly re-qualify yourself as an expert in your given marketplace, while making people aware that you have done so.

The Art of Consulting – a Delicate Balance

Considering all of the requirements, it is clear that being a successful consultant is quite demanding. However, I believe the true art to a successful consulting career is finding a balance between your personal life and your professional life. The balance isn't the same for everybody. Each individual has to find what works for him or her. Everyone has a different comfort level and is in a different position with respect to his or her life cycle. You cannot and should not impose your values and balance on other individuals. You have to let each consultant find his or her own comfort level. As a consultant, you need to understand what is important to you as an individual. You have to recognize that every volleyball game you miss or every gymnastics meet that you can't make is a missed opportunity that may not come around again. You have to make judgment calls. There are tradeoffs you will face. There are times in every consultant's life when you are stuck somewhere, and there are family events you are going to miss. You have to assign an appropriate level of importance to those personal obligations and opportunities, just as you do to meetings with your clients. The fact is most clients understand that you cannot be available during certain periods of time, and they are willing to schedule around those events. Balance is the key to a long-term consulting career.

Success

When do you know you are successful as a consultant? Generally, you know you are successful if, upon completion of a given assignment, the client asks you another question or gives you another assignment. Generally, if they are asking another question, they are happy with your work. If they stop asking questions, or start directing those questions to others, there is a reasonable chance that you have not completed your assignment successfully. If the client is comfortable with you, has confidence in you, and believes you are capable of answering a particular question, then they will continue to seek your counsel.

Having said that, there are times when a client asks a consultant what he or she thinks, and once told, the client will disagree. As a consultant, you cannot take that disagreement personally. You have to remember that you are not always right and that clients have the right to be wrong. You have to allow clients to make their own choices based upon the information they have and the input you give them. If they act in a way that is contrary to the advice you have given them, you have to accept that they may know more than you about a particular aspect of their decision. Or you may be right, and they may be wrong. You have to let them be wrong at times. Some of my most loyal clients have been clients who have disagreed with me from time to time.

If you are going to be a successful consultant, you have to add value in multiples of your fees. It's not enough to add value equal to your fee; you have to add value well in excess of your fee – three, five, ten times your fee. As your clients gain confidence in your ability to add value, you will be asked broader questions with respect to their business.

Many times a client knows he needs help but does not know what question he should ask. These assignments can be the most fulfilling, because they allow the consultant to add substantial value. One of the most critical skills needed to be a successful consultant is the ability to listen. When a client does not know what the question is, your ability to listen and abstract from him or her what the issues are can be one of your most valuable contributions. Obviously, once you identify the questions or issues facing your client, you can then proceed to providing solutions.

Staying in touch with other consultants, as well as others in your profession, by participating in industry meetings and on committees is another important component of a successful consulting career. I have personally written a number of papers and have spoken at a number of industry-wide meetings. Consultants have asked me if I think these activities translate into the development of more business. I typically answer that I don't know for sure, but I would not want to risk the growth I have experienced by not writing or speaking. Likewise, staying involved contributes to the value you add to your given profession, even if you can't be sure it contributes to your commercial success.

In the consulting business, results speak for themselves. If a consultant keeps his or her existing clients happy and grows his or her client base over the long term, that is *a priori* evidence that he or she is successful. A consultant who is willing to listen and not impose his or her will in the first five minutes of a conversation, and who can articulate his or her conclusions based upon an understanding of the issues the clients are confronting, typically will be a successful consultant. A consultant who understands the need to listen, the ability to communicate, and the need to reinvest in his or her knowledge base will typically be successful over the long term.

No Cookie-Cutter Solutions

Another ramification of the question "What do you think?" is that you *have* to think. There are no cookie-cutter solutions anymore. The world has become too complicated. Everyone's issues are different. Your ability to listen and extract those issues is critical to your success as a consultant.

To a great extent, consulting involves addressing client issues on an 80/20 basis. They want you to answer 80 percent of the question in 20 percent of the time. There are very few times in consulting when you will get to the absolute completion of a project. This also has implications for the way you perform your job. You have to have expertise in the topic you are consulting on before you enter into an assignment. You will tailor-make the answer to the specific company's issues, but you have to have a very broad knowledge base. You need the basic background ahead of time. If you are not well prepared to answer the question your client is asking before they ask, you will probably not receive the assignment. Advance preparation is the key.

I am a firm believer in strong fundamentals. If you are not fundamentally sound, whether in an athletic endeavor or in your business practices, your performance will be flawed, and ultimately you will not excel. Those who are fundamentally sound, who are capable of blocking and tackling, and who are willing to prepare in advance will be the individuals who succeed over the long run. Then, the only thing more difficult than *reaching* the top is *remaining* on top. You have to do all of the things you did to get there, and then do some more. There is always somebody who wants to replace you. Maintaining strong fundamentals leads to continued success.

Communication Is Fundamental

The ability to communicate effectively, in writing and orally, is absolutely necessary if you are to become a first-rate consultant. All too often I meet students who are lacking in one or the other of these basic skills. You can be the smartest person, but if you can't communicate to your clients what you think about an issue, you will not succeed as a consultant. Good communication skills are not only a necessary attribute for a successful consultant, but they are also one of the most critical skills.

I will admit to a bias. I am a voracious reader, and I firmly believe that reading everything I can get my hands on has assisted me greatly in my consulting career. Consultants need to anticipate the questions their clients ask. One way to anticipate questions is to read. Reading should make up a large component of any consultant's time. It helps a consultant gain insight into business as a whole, as well as the particular businesses to which they are consulting. Read about questions that companies are asking in other countries, because those are questions that may be asked in the United States. Read about industries that are not now the focus of your consulting practice. There are legislative, regulatory, environmental, and business issues affecting industries you don't typically consult to that may help you address questions your clients may eventually ask. Reading will also help you improve and refine your communication skills. Reading is a key requisite for keeping your edge.

Opportunities

Sometimes a down economic environment creates a greater need for consultants. Consultants may be brought in to do the work that internal staff would have done prior to a downsizing. Clients hire consultants when they need them and fire them when they don't. Consulting is a variable cost as opposed to a fixed cost, and a down economy can create opportunities for consultants.

Likewise, there are a lot of questions faced by clients that consultants can address when business isn't going well. As a consultant, therefore, you have to position yourself to answer questions in both up and down markets.

Best Advice

Our firm, Milliman USA, is now over 50 years old. The best piece of business advice I ever received was that each Milliman consultant should view the firm as a tool – a tool to be used to add value to your clients and reach your personal and professional goals. However, just as when your grandfather took a tool off of his workbench, sharpened it, oiled it, used it, and then replaced it, you need to leave the tool (*i.e.,* your consulting firm) in better shape than when you found it. If every consultant in your firm takes that kind of ownership and makes that kind of commitment, then you will clearly have a growing, profitable, successful firm over a long period of time.

When consultants in other firms don't serve their clients well, it hurts all consultants. Likewise, when consultants perform well, the pie gets larger for all consultants. You should always strive to give the client more than he or she expects. On any given assignment, whether it is a fixed-fee or a time-and-expense-fee job, always give the client more than is expected.

Firm Structure

A firm's organizational structure, ownership structure, and culture dictate what kind of people will be comfortable and successful there. For instance, Milliman USA is a firm in which we have multiple profit centers. The profit centers are merely a mechanism for splitting up the pie at the end of the day. However, they have contributed to the creation of a firm that is the ultimate meritocracy. We have consultants who are relatively young who are compensated more than consultants who are older and have been with the firm for a longer period of time. The contribution you make in any given period determines your compensation. This goes from the equity principals of the firm all the way down through the clerical staff. Because of this organizational structure, we tend to attract very entrepreneurial and aggressive individuals.

Consulting is a relatively simple business. It is not a capital-intensive business. Our assets are our people. Our focus is on getting the people who will best address the questions and issues our clients face. We believe our ownership and organizational structure allows us to attract the very best people.

The consulting firms that succeed in the long run are the ones that attract the highest caliber people. I believe firms that are owned and operated by their consultants are well positioned for the future because they will, in the long run, attract a disproportionate share of the best people. Consultants who own the firm participate in the ownership return, as well as the return generated by their consultative efforts.

To illustrate, let's assume you are a consultant considering joining Firm A or Firm B. Firm A allows you to extract the ownership return; whereas, Firm B has sold the ownership return to external owners, whether through a public offering or to another firm. I believe the best people will be attracted to Firm A because they will be compensated for their efforts more directly, and will participate in the ownership return.

The Consulting Environment

Technology has made consulting easier, as well as more difficult. Although technology cuts down on the amount of time it takes to complete an assignment, it has also increased client expectations (sometimes unreasonably) with respect to the amount of time needed to complete a given assignment. The pace of consulting, partially because of technology, is much faster than it used to be. The questions are changing at a faster pace, and technology has created higher expectations.

It is important to understand the market for which you want to consult, as well as its expectations. An analogy exists with retailers. On one extreme, in the retail marketplace, you have Wal-Mart, which is very successful in the market they serve. They are very successful doing what they do best, selling high-quantity, low-margin items. On the other hand, there is Nordstrom. They are a high-value-added, high-margin operation. It has been said that if you walk into a Nordstrom at 8:55 p.m., five minutes before they close, and you need a pair of shoes, they will stay open as long as necessary for you to pick out those shoes, because that is their business.

Typically, consultants are high-value-added, high-margin businesses. If your consulting firm wants to be a high-value-added business, you need to understand the requirements of that model. The implications are that, if a client calls you at 5:30 on Friday afternoon and wants you to complete an assignment and deliver it to them by 8:30 on Monday morning, you need to be willing to work on Saturday and Sunday to complete that project. That does not mean you will work every Saturday and Sunday. It just means that you have to be willing to work on Saturday and Sunday if that is what is necessary to complete an assignment to your client's satisfaction. Likewise, you do not have to work until 10:00 every night. But when a client asks you to do that, or satisfactory completion of an assignment demands it, you have to be willing to invest the time because, otherwise, you are not a high-value-added consultant. You have to make the commitment to be available on short notice 24 hours a day, seven days a week. That doesn't mean you have to work those hours – that is clearly impossible. But you have to be available when your clients want you.

Consulting is a client service business, and all consultants need to understand that. If we do not keep our clients happy, we are not going to stay in business very long.

It is important to understand your goals as an individual consultant, as well as your firm's goals. I am not a big fan of short-term goal setting. I think it is more important to focus on long-term goals and address where you want to be as an individual and as a firm, three years from now, five years from now, ten years from now. If you understand where you want to be in five or ten years, the short-term tactics seem apparent. At times, people make mistakes when they over-emphasize short-term goals, thereby doing something to meet a specific short-term goal that they wouldn't do otherwise.

This has ramifications in choosing the clients you work for. You have to discriminate between those clients for whom you believe you can add value and those for whom you can't. If you don't think you can add value for a potential client, you need to pass on that opportunity. If you are too focused on short-term revenue or growth goals, it may lead to a bad decision with regard to accepting an assignment where you cannot add value.

I think more people are going to enter the consulting field because industry is attempting to lower fixed costs and, consequently, will reduce staff positions. Industry will continue to reduce fixed staff costs, transforming them into variable consulting costs. Therefore, I believe the consulting industry will grow substantially over the next decade.

The consulting industry is constantly challenged by the litigious society in which we operate. The answer you gave as a consultant may have been well thought out and the appropriate answer at a given time, but three to five months later, in retrospect, it may prove to have not been the right answer. That does not mean that the advice given at the time was bad, or constituted malpractice, or necessarily was actionable from a legal standpoint. Consultants cannot be the ultimate reinsurer of any particular outcome for their clients. There must be an understanding or recognition of this fact if consulting is to continue as a viable profession over the long run. Ultimately, management needs to accept the responsibility for what it thinks is appropriate while considering the consultant's advice. The biggest threat to the consulting industry right now is the rise in litigation. In fact, this is not a risk that can be accepted by consulting firms or a cost that can be transferred economically to the client. You have to recognize and accept what consulting is and what it is not.

None of us lives in a vacuum. When momentous events on the world stage alter business as we know it, there will have to be a consequential impact on the advice we give to our clients. A substantial core of the business of Milliman USA involves the development of projections. These include projections of net income and cash flow projections for insurance companies, pension and other employee benefit costs, and liabilities for all types of enterprises, as well as demographic projections for governmental entities.

World events, as they unfold, will certainly have an impact on the work we do and the advice we give to our clients. Maintaining and enhancing our relevance to the markets we serve is the biggest challenge faced by any consultant or professional consulting firm. Maintaining relevance involves the identification of areas in which the skills of the consultant can be utilized to add value in multiples for the client. Once identified, the consultant must have or develop the capabilities and do the research that will allow him or her to add value to their clients and potential clients.

One of the dangers faced by all consultants is that while they are working on projects, satisfying the current demands of their clients, they do not invest the time or resources necessary to maintain relevance in the future. Specifically, they do not invest in their knowledge base; they lose touch with their marketplace; they fail to do the research necessary to serve their marketplace tomorrow, next month, next quarter, next year.

The Golden Rules of Consulting

The golden rules of consulting are:

1)   Always give clients more than they expect.
2)   Make sure you understand where you as a consultant and your firm want to go in the long run.
3)   Maintain balance in your life consistent with what makes you happy.
4)   Continuously reinvest in your knowledge and experience base, recognizing that these are constantly amortizing assets.
5)   Most importantly, have fun while you are doing it.

Bradley M. Smith graduated from the University of Illinois in 1977 with highest honors.

Mr. Smith is a Fellow of the Society of Actuaries, a member of the American Academy of Actuaries, and a Fellow of the Life Management Institute (LOMA). He formerly served on the Board of Governors of the Society of Actuaries. He joined Milliman & Robertson, Inc., now known as Milliman USA, in April 1986 to open the life/health practice in Dallas. His practice involves all aspects of life and health insurance, including insurance industry mergers and acquisitions, product pricing, and financial statement preparation. He served as a member of Milliman's board of directors from May 1996 to May 1999. In May 2000 he was elected to the position of Milliman USA chairman of the board of directors.

Before joining Milliman, Mr. Smith was vice president and chief actuary at JCPenney Life Insurance Company, where he was heavily involved in direct-response marketing analysis, list segmentation, product development, and corporate planning.

Before working at JCPenney Life, Mr. Smith worked in the product development and the reinsurance departments at Republic National Life.

TAILORING SOLUTIONS TO MEET CLIENT NEEDS

THOMAS J. SILVERI

Drake Beam Morin

Chief Executive Officer and President

The Art of Consulting

I've been involved in the industry, in one form or another, for 20 years. I started with Price Waterhouse in public accounting – an excellent base on which to learn. After Price Waterhouse I spent a decade in the advertising and public relations business in various finance and administrative positions. Now I'm with Drake Beam Morin, the world's leading career transition consulting firm, and serve as the company's president and CEO.

I've always been in the personal services business. The personal service sector is really what gives me the charge. Everything is grounded in good educational background in theory, but in practice, one needs to have an active listening skill and be able to adapt that book knowledge and knowledge gained from experience, and implement it through effective solutions that work for the customers. I always find that to be the most exciting part of the job. Everything has to be tailored to meet their needs and where they, as an organization, want to go.

You're always dealing with different people; you're always dealing with unique challenges. The "solution set" for a customer is never really the same, nor should it be. You get to deal with the human capital element, which is something every consultant really does. If you want to do your job well as a consultant, you'd better like working with people;

you'd better like that interface; and you'd better be a good listener to be able to impart your knowledge in a way that will be accepted by those you're consulting with. For me, that has always been the biggest reward. I enjoy it and have stayed in it my whole career. I would urge anyone who wants to get into business today and loves interpersonal interaction to take a look at the consulting sector as a career path.

The art of consulting requires mastering the art of listening to a set of problems that an organization or individuals have, quickly and efficiently assessing where the organization is, and developing a rational approach to getting where the organization wants to go. It also requires that you make sure the solution set you provide is in keeping with the organization's culture, its needs, its directions, and its competencies. If you're successful in doing that, you'll be able to move the agenda of those you're working for more quickly and efficiently in the constantly changing world of work.

Another integral part of the job is that the customers will often look to you as the solution to the problem, when in fact you're the facilitator to that solution. Customers tend to have the feeling that once they've turned a problem over, then the problem is just going to get solved. That's something we have to manage on the front end. From our perspective, the most important part of active listening is understanding the customer's expectation and managing that early on as it relates to what is possible and what we can deliver – and never, ever over-promise. Your credibility is on the line, and the organization that's hiring you is on the line, and the investment is on the line, so never over-promise and under-deliver.

Defining success in consulting depends on the role and whom you're talking to. From my perspective in my role as CEO, as the leader of a consulting company, I define success as being able to have the company execute as many of our recommendations and procedures as possible in a way that ultimately moves their agenda forward.

Success for me is repeat business. Success for me is the moving forward of that organization's agenda through the use of our time and our resources. And of course, speaking as a CEO, we want to do that in a way that is profitable. We want to do it in a way that allows for the growth and development of our people and our practice, so we can constantly be moving forward and be at the forefront of whatever is coming next. My best definition of success is repeat customer activity; it means that we have secured a relationship with a customer where we have provided a value-added contribution, and they want to use us again.

Methodologies

In general, as we go about the sales process, we are constantly using specialists in an attempt to provide a value-add to our customer base and understand enough about that customer base to quickly bring our value-add to the table. From our perspective at DBM, we spend a significant amount of time behind the scenes, talking about the competencies to which we can provide a value-add solution set. The goal is not to focus on that competency that you can't provide value-add quickly and efficiently. No customer wants to pay for your learning, nor should they.

At DBM, we religiously focus on where we have the skill set and match that quickly with industries and solution-set methodologies so we can provide that value-add to the customer. Then, when you have that opportunity after you've identified that solution set, you've identified the competency and skill set you bring. You want to make sure you know enough about that customer to be able to clearly understand and precisely articulate that solution set early enough in the process, so there's a degree of comfort. That's the way to be successful.

We've spent a lot of time internally describing who we are and who we are not. I do think that matters very much to organizations today. They need to know that you provide a value-add immediately to the process. If you start there and say, "We can do this, and we can do that, and by the way, we can handle that as well," I think you'll immediately "turn off" customers. Customers look for value-add, and they look for a specific set of solutions, and they want you to immediately articulate that in a way that brings a solution to the table. We spend a lot of time doing that, and I think we're successful as a result.

We don't want to be everything to everybody. There are times when we'll turn down business, or we'll refer business to others because we know what we can do, and we know what we can't do. As a consultant you need to sit down with your own strategy, with your own direction, and assess your own skill set first. If you know where you can provide that value-add and know where you can play because you have the internal resources to do that, then you set up your business strategies that way. If you can convince yourself and your people you have the "permission" to effectively bring a solution to the marketplace, and you have that internal mindset in place, you can easily convince the customer. If you don't, you will wallow around in the world of consulting and not be very successful.

We focus a lot of our energy into really strengthening relationships, so that DBM is a truly reliable and trustworthy partner. Given the nature of our business, a lot of what we do and say is sensitive – we deal with company culture issues, which we all know gets at the structural foundations of an organization. The strength and depth of our one-on-one relationships with our customers are really keyed around success. Often, our customers are traumatized by the types of initiatives they need to implement when we engage with them to get them through restructuring exercises or laying off workers. We need to know their agenda and find out its impact on them as individuals, because this will ultimately affect how they're going to do the job.

Providing Value-add

Providing value-add is a process you need to follow through within your own strategic planning. It involves talking about where you provide that skill set. Let me give you an example: We represent several companies in the high-tech business that are going through considerable restructurings at this time. That gives us the opportunity to work with a variety of customers, many of whom have similar, though not exactly the same, challenges. What we do is pull from our knowledge base. We have people who have worked on those programs and know exactly what that market is and how we can best provide that value-add to the customer in that market and how we can best secure career transitions for their employee base. When we've accumulated our knowledge and identified our strengths, the execution of the knowledge to the customer is easy.

When we approach a high-tech company, we're not going in saying, "We're the leading consultants on career transition issues." We go in and say, "We understand the problems surrounding the placement of employees within this industry and the potential path result because of these issues. Here are the solutions that we've thought through as to why it makes sense to engage in this way." I think only when you do this do you secure revenue growth and customer acceptance.

We spend a lot of time in the planning process fostering that understanding of our skills internally, selling it to ourselves. And if we can sell it to ourselves, we know we can be the best at convincing our customers. We're able to answer many of the questions our customers have before we walk into that first meeting.

Getting up to speed requires a front-end approach. Our consultants must do a considerable amount of work before they walk into any request for proposal (RFP) or any presentation made in front of a customer. This involves learning as much as they can about the company through public sources, as well as gathering information in the pre-interview process, where we sit down and identify needs and outcomes with the individuals who asked us to come in. Even before we walk in that door, though, we want to have a good sense of the company's issues and what the company expects of that meeting.

Our management requires this front-end investigatory process by our consultants. We have processes that help facilitate that information gathering: Consultants can use our databases of information to immediately track down historical data or information about career transition trends in the industry. It is important to have those systems in place in your organization, so your people can be most effective in the execution of their sales endeavors.

We would not let any of our team go into any presentation without having completed the front-end process. If we did that, we wouldn't be successful.

Pitfalls and Golden Rules

In my experience in consulting, I have found a direct correlation between the number of people in front of the customer and the profitability of the firm. What that essentially means is you want to put all of your company's efforts and resources toward the customer in the form of face-to-face contact, and marketing and sales activities and external research in the form of continued development. You do not put your resources into internal office space or elaborate internal systems. If you keep your back office to a minimum, always provide an external focus to your meetings, and limit your internal process meetings, you will be successful. I think those who are not successful in the consulting arena view their company as a "big organization," where an "entitlement" culture is allowed to exist. I think that is a major pitfall in consulting.

The best business advice I can give is the more people on the line in front of the customer, the better. You have to understand ultimately that your business is driven by the value-add contribution you give to the customer; all other activities around that should be geared toward that customer. If you keep your focus on that, you'll be successful. That's how we've built our company.

At DBM we have "six imperatives" that we filter through every business decision we make:

1. Share a common vision worldwide.
2. Think and act globally.
3. See through the eyes of the customer or client.
4. Maximize employee talent.
5. Leverage technology.
6. Have a sense of urgency and purpose.

If any decision cannot easily be seen through the eyes of the customer as a value-add, then we don't do it. This doesn't mean we don't have equipment that allows people to do their jobs, but by the same token, we don't want to have a sense of value internally that is not generated by the external marketplace. People have to have the tools to do their jobs, but if you are doing something or buying something just to keep someone's title or exclusively for the profitability of the company, you will not be successful.

Also, I'm going to mention again the hazard of focusing on what you can't do. I think a lot of effort is expended on creating solutions that aren't core to what companies do. By forming a planning platform, we do stay focused as an organization on our core competencies. We meet regularly and constantly challenge ourselves to "re-test" our thinking. I think any organization that wants to be successful really needs to do that. It's extraordinarily rare to see a consulting organization that is able to play in the full spectrum of potential consulting advice and counsel. They may play in other arenas, but they have a specific skill set they focus on and move forward with. A smaller company would be wise to limit themselves, to pinpoint the value-add situations they can really play in, as opposed to saying, "I can be your consultant."

Never play in an area where you don't have the value-add contribution thought through in advance. Never over-commit to a customer your ability to deliver the product you suggest. Never surprise a company with the amount of a bill or how you're executing the program. Over-deliver, as opposed to under-deliver, and stay in touch. Whether or not you've completed the assignment, maintain and develop that relationship because you never know when that will come back.

Managing In Turbulent Times

I'm in a different business from a traditional consulting perspective in that our business is helping people through career change. As such, at times of economic change, particularly when world economies are in recession, our activities are extremely brisk. In fact, we could almost be called a counter-cyclical service in that there is more need for our assistance when the economy is not doing well, as organizations are realizing the need to right-size or align their workforces with their declining revenue streams. Conversely, we have turbulent times when the economy is so strong that there is not as much support around career transition, or organizations aren't taking people out. We can understand that, but then we have to ask how can we help in those situations? Where will our skill set apply when it is not in demand in a given economic climate? Our strength is not just in career transitions; it is about supplying support and counsel around HR solutions to the market.

To enhance this, we've used many of the programs we've implemented for career-transitioned employees to help organizations when they're going through change that might not actually involve career transitions – for example, executive coaching or retention issues, which are areas in which we have the competencies to play. We already have the skill set and the solution set we need to provide. I think, as an organization, you need to be balanced in product or service and customers. In turbulent times we do quite well, and when the economy is good, we balance that with the customer need. That means helping organizations with change.

We've looked at our organizational resources, and we know where we are strong in that arena: For us it's in retention and executive coaching, areas where we can provide value-add. Organizations that struggle need to refocus their business quickly, then think about their core competencies and what the consumer is looking for, then gear their service where they already have strength in that competency. Companies need to be fast and fluid with that. It is important to look at yourself as a small company, no matter what the size, because then you can provide quick solutions when you have an area of crisis. DBM is a $300 million company today, and it operates as a $20 million company. We're fast, and we'll make changes as needed by the marketplace. No consulting company will be successful long-term unless it has that ability to change.

The People

For an individual to be successful, you need to have a broad experience base and strong interpersonal skills. You need a well-rounded individual who has the desire and the ability to communicate, to listen, and to react, and the ability to do that in a way that is driven by the best interest of the customer. I'm looking for people who have a strong overall skill set around written or oral communication. I'm looking for people who want to do something different and provide change. Those people are motivated and therefore successful.

As a leader whose experiences are developed through the personal services sector industry, that's how I was brought up. I am not interested in sitting in on internal meetings, trying to move my career forward that way. I'd rather be out in front of the customer. I enjoy that, whether it's on a personal level, a customer relationship level, or an external practice development level, or whether it's a tradeshow or new business. But you have to want to interrelate. It is your job "satisfier." If you don't want that interaction, then the consulting business is not for you. If you stay in the business without this ability to interrelate, and enjoy it, you'll have a rather limited role within the consulting organization. You need to have communication skills, whether oral or written, and an intense desire to help people look forward.

Our best consultants have the intense desire to execute with the customer. They are responsive to their needs in a way that makes the customer feel as though they're "part of the company" instead of in a "vendor" relationship. I've seen some excellent presentations and some excellent executions that haven't been customer focused, where the presenter used a book solution or a solution set thought through by a very well educated individual, but these were not worked through with the customer in a way that the company understood and could execute on it.

The best consultants are those who understand they can work through the company, and know that it is their responsibility to get in there with the company in helping to execute those solutions. They care about that company, care about their responsibility in the process, and work with the management of the company. They have to execute that strategy and stay engaged, even after the experience. Those who are good consultants probably have the right answer, and have come up with good strategic thought around their solution, but they don't understand the culture or the nuance of the person paying for the service, and as a result, they don't provide the type of support necessary to get the program through.

At DBM we think of ourselves as a leading-edge learning organization. One of our criteria is to have a desire and personal responsibility to grow professionally. You need to devote a period of time to becoming state-of-the-art to forward your career. At DBM we know we're dealing with highly talented people in this organization, and we want and need to drive them toward their own development and desires and a continued learning situation, so we provide funds to that end and train along those lines. To be successful in the business, you need to have that same mindset. Your job is not just to execute well today; your job is to execute today and learn about today's challenges, so you can address tomorrow's solutions. The best people who do that do it on their own time, as well as on company time. They do that in a way they find constructive, whether it's a specific industry or a specific weakness they want to address. They need to do that to be successful.

Personally, I accomplish this balance by rigorously maintaining two non-work facets of my life: I take time to get away from the business occasionally, and I work hard at balancing my business and family time. I like to take one week off every three months, where I can get away and sit and think and read. I put this week in my book and make sure my secretary doesn't fill that time slot. I need time outside of the day-to-day rush to think of where the business is going and where it can best be supported going forward. I would urge all employees to do something like that. Taking a day off here or there, or every Friday in the summer will not be enough to get you to "see the forest through the trees." That's how I handle my long-term needs. For me, balance of life is important, and to give myself that extra time, I just go in very early in the morning. Sometimes I'm in my office by 6:30 a.m., and I get home late at night. I work on my e-mails at night. When I'm there, I'm there. But when I am gone, I'm gone.

Also, my children are extraordinarily important to me in achieving balance in my life. I will leave at three in the afternoon on days my son plays baseball for his high school varsity team. I will go there, take out my lawn chair, and sit and watch him play, and from 4 p.m., when his game starts, until 6 p.m., when it's over, I have the phone off. I'm just sitting there, watching the game, watching my son – that gives me the balance. It doesn't bother me to be at work early or to be working on e-mail at 10:00 at night. But for me, that time with my son is important and I will take that time. I would advise every person in an organization to find that balance. People can do that differently in different organizations. Some people get up early; some people turn off the computer and leave. That's it for their night. Some leave the weekends for themselves. The methodology is not important; the result is.

The Future of Consulting

You're going to see a continued explosion in the consulting business in the next five to ten years. More and more companies are going to outsource what they can. They're going to be looking for a specific expertise to drive their organizations forward, and they're not inclined to have that sitting in their organization.

As organizations adapt, recombine, and merge, this will be the business to be in, both today and in the future. You will continue to see an explosion in this industry as organizations are more inclined to get that specific data that they need when they need it. Organizations will be willing to pay a premium for it, as opposed to keeping a workforce on a fixed basis to get it day-in and day-out.

Do I think the business is a good one? You bet. Do I think it's growing? Absolutely! I see all the corporate dynamics being in favor of consulting organizations growing and growing. Take, for example, the talents and skill sets that are necessary for today's solutions. They are more complicated today and very often cross-functional. No one alone can create the solutions – only the appropriate environment for the team to reach an appropriate solution.

There is also no question that the demographics of people who are leaving the workforce will leave spaces that the organizations will have to fill. Organizations can fill those spaces internally, or they can look externally, and the trend is that they will look externally. People are less inclined to be tied to one organization and more inclined to be responsible for their own careers, and they can do that much more easily in a consulting environment than in one organization. The increasing trend of working out of your home, or telecommuting, will play a role in leading consulting organizations going forward. The consulting business is going to continue to expand in the upcoming years, and I'm glad to be a part of this exciting and vibrant industry.

Thomas J. Silveri is chief executive officer and president of Drake Beam Morin (DBM), a position he assumed in April 2000. He is responsible for handling the day-to-day management of the company's global operations.

Before assuming this role, Mr. Silveri was chief operating officer of DBM's U.S. operations. He also previously held the position of senior vice president, finance and administration, where he was responsible for DBM's accounting department, the financial planning and analysis group, information systems, and facilities management functions.

Before joining DBM in 1993, Mr. Silveri obtained 13 years of experience in specialized fields of the media business – public relations, advertising, and research. Previously, Mr. Silveri was executive vice president, finance and administration, at Hill and Knowlton, and prior to that, he was controller of JWT Group.

THE FUTURE OF MARKETING CONSULTING

DAVID FRIGSTAD

Frost & Sullivan

Chairman

The Direction of Marketing Consulting

The future of the marketing consulting industry looks very positive as many trends and technologies come together to enhance the relationship between the consultant and the client. On the information side, we see an accelerating integration of the Internet with competitive intelligence, CRM, market intelligence, and KMS. This integration, combined with an increasing demand for ethics in market and competitive data collection, will support companies in their efforts to outsource strategic information-gathering and strategy formulation to their primary consultants. The relationship between consultant and client will become much more seamless in the future as information is shared among all players in given projects, including the global enterprise and the external partners, which include the consultants.

A vast number of emerging and disruptive technologies in a rapidly globalizing economy will significantly increase the demand for multi-talented consulting teams, which possess many specific skills to make projects successful. The traditional internal teams will not have the skill sets to perform successful global projects in a time frame to meet financial success. The demand for specialized market and technical consultants, working in close cooperation and in strict confidentiality with the clients, will be much more common in coming years. There appear to be very few consulting companies ready for this transition.

Exciting Things About Consulting

What is a tremendous amount of fun is working with different executives with completely different cultural backgrounds. One day you're in Germany; the next day you're in China; and then you're in Japan.

Everyday everyone looks at business with a different perspective, and when you go into those kinds of challenges, it's really a great pleasure to learn about other cultures and meet other people. It's hard to say why it's so exciting, but that cross-cultural interaction is a lot of fun and very rewarding.

Changes in the Business Environment

The biggest single shift in the business environment is toward globalization. I started in 1980, and when I had a project in Germany, it was about the German market. If I had a project in Japan, it was about the Japanese market. It was always very regionally focused. Now 75 percent of our clients come to us, and they want every region of the world covered. That just wasn't happening ten years ago. This trend toward globalization means that as a consulting company, we have to completely reconfigure our global team of analysts, the specialties they have, and even the make-up of who they are. Years ago, probably 95 percent of our staff were American or British, and today less than half of our staff was born in the United States. You really need that multi-cultural focus in the business because clients are asking what's going on in all these different countries.

The second biggest change is the Internet. The Internet has given clients an incredible leap in value-add because of the integration of knowledge management techniques and principles, which you simply couldn't do on paper.

It's going to be very interesting because the Internet is causing a very pure flow of information that we have never had before. When the world was based on paper, there were a lot of papers on which large consulting companies could draw. Suddenly, the Internet puts large consulting companies at great risk. Now a client looking for a specific technology in a specific issue can go to the Internet and be exposed to hundreds of companies that are very focused on their need. They will not be forced to go to the large brand-name consulting companies to get their intelligence. I think one result of this is that fragmentation in the business might happen and have a huge impact. The large companies will grow more slowly, and there will be many more boutique firms going forward. At least there's a big risk of that happening.

Another big trend is toward a more integrated approach for client applications. I see that a lot of our clients are very frustrated because they get customer information and market share information from the companies that are polling the customer base. Then they're getting their market information and analysis and strategy from Frost and Sullivan. They get their regulatory news and government news from a newsletter. They get econometric data and economic forecasts from other suppliers, and they get customer demographic information from other companies beyond that. None of this information is integrated, even though it correlates very well. Customers don't have time to make sense of all this different data. The great pressure going forward will be to integrate all of this information into something that holds together and can be leveraged to help a client create a strategy. When Frost and Sullivan was founded, we just focused on competitive data. Then we started our customer survey centers to collect data. Now we're looking very closely at econometric forecasts and data by industry. We're adding demographic tables and are integrating all of this information so it makes sense, so it's not conflicting, and so our clients can use it rapidly. I think there will be a trend toward clients wanting consultants that integrate a broader spectrum of the information, as well as the strategy.

What Success Means

Good marketing consulting is very much focused on the marketing aspect of a client's portfolio. When I sit down with my long-term clients, we go through all the projects we've done, and a lot of what we do is work on new product development and product launches and things of that nature. We see success in terms of killing a bad idea or making a new product launch more effective. Clients sometimes have a hard time relating to stopping an R&D project and seeing it as great success. The point here is that stopping bad ideas is a success, even though they have to write down quite a bit of R&D investment. But we go back and look at the ROI on the project, including the future expenses on the project, and we can see the positive return of stopping what doesn't make sense, just as we can for promoting something that does make sense.

Measuring success can be a difficult thing to do, however. When consultants more and more become partners with our larger clients, when you're working very closely with their marketing associates, their CEOs, and their business development executives in a partnership, it becomes a little harder to measure success. Even though you know you can speed up their decisions, integrate information for them better, and provide new insights and strategies, at the end of the day, it's a smile on the face of the CEO and the stakeholder that tells you you're on the right track.

Measuring marketing consulting success has become a lot harder over time because the clients' expectations for the integration of data, for knowledge management, and for helping with the implementation have all increased significantly. The client teams have gotten larger. In the past we would deal with one person in one company. Now we're suddenly dealing with a global team of project development managers. It's harder to measure success because you're trying to keep 12 people integrated, happy, and satisfied with what you're doing instead of just one. It has definitely gotten harder to measure success, to know that what you're doing is right, and it has put a lot of pressure on other companies to be constantly improving. What we're doing today is at least twice as good as what we were doing five years ago, but I think all the consulting companies are following that track, as well.

Opportunities for Consulting

A lot of opportunity sits in application consulting, which is studying the job functions within a client and understanding them enough to make a particular executive more powerful in their impact on the company. You really have to first understand the objectives of that executive's title and then the applications that go along with those objectives. You need to have a consulting methodology for each of the applications. What I often see is the same research design and methodology applied to any application. But applications are different, and you don't get as accurate results or as good strategies emanating from a one-size-fits-all approach.

One way to realize the opportunity is to really fine-tune the consulting process for a specific application. I think that's probably a very difficult thing to do (as we're learning ourselves), but it's really great once you get on top of it. One example is in acquisitions. Most companies do a very poor job of conducting due diligence on acquisitions. They do a very poor job of understanding an acquisition's position within the customer group and within the landscape. A more specific methodology of analyzing those things just for the application of acquisitions will increase the company's success rate of doing that. I see most consulting firms using the same methodology, regardless of the challenge, but the real opportunity is to develop expertise in each one of the applications.

Successful Methodologies

If you know what the application is, you'll know where you should go after it. At the beginning, you either identify a challenge for a client, or what their key application is going to be. Once that's identified, you have to find out the most pertinent data to address that challenge. This is where I think a lot of consultants fall apart. Say you're launching a new technology. At some level, it's very important to get the proper data from the entire client population, or at least a statistically significant sample size. It depends on how you segment the client population as part of the methodology, and most importantly what questions to ask and in what forum to ask them. These are often done on Internet surveys or by telephone surveys. Depending on the application, you might need to go out and do face-to-face surveys, or you might need to look at focus groups. If there are five or six different ways to segment a client population, there are five or six different research instruments to get information from the population. In addition, if you're working in customer groups, there is the competitive landscape, and then there's the regulatory landscape to add to the mix. There are a lot more options and permutations to look at when you're trying to solve this problem, but you could end up using five or six methodologies, depending on the application.

One of the methods we really specialize in is getting the right information from the client base, but not only on the product we're looking at. We also look for the competitor products and disruptive technologies to really round out the whole spectrum of strategic options.

One methodology we have found useful for quite a few of our clients is using a measurement like brand recognition.

Today there's an increased emphasis on brand recognition and equity and brand value. We go out for our clients and interview the competitor's clients and their customers, and we'll ask questions about brand recognition and brand recall. We find that with some of our largest clients, their customers cannot remember their company's name or the product. This can really shock a client because the tendency within a company, if you have a successful product, is that your arrogance grows and grows to a point where you can become completely blind to what's going on in the marketplace. But if you look at a brand value – that is, going out and looking at a diverse section of the consumer database – you can come back with a reality check of where the brand really is. That has provided tremendous value for a lot of clients because they suddenly realize that they thought they were at point A, and they're actually at point C. It creates value-added discussions and strategies to get them back on track.

Keeping Pace with the Markets

I think we have a tremendous advantage because we employ over 700 analysts who track nine different industrial sectors full-time. If you're constantly talking to the vendors, talking to the customers, and talking to regulators in probably 20 countries around the world, you can keep pace with what is going on. That helps you keep

focused on the strategic challenges that we'll be facing –
such as the consolidation of the pharmaceutical industry,
generic pharmaceuticals, and the current global economic
recession.

By studying those analyses when we go to see a CEO or a
VP of business development, we already have information
that we know will be keeping them up at 4:00 in the
morning thinking about it. You can't go into a client and
ask, "What kind of consulting needs do you have today?"
You have to go in and say, "We'd like to talk to you about
how your company is addressing this problem, this
challenge, or this opportunity." That usually gets a very
positive response because it's a multi-million dollar or
billion-dollar impact on that company.

The Differences Among Consulting Companies

There are different types of consulting. There has certainly
been a huge boom in the IT consulting and implementation
end of the business in recent years, and I don't really put
that in the realm of what we do. That boom has made
companies like Accenture very successful.

Then you have the management consultants, like
Booz·Allen and McKenzie. And then there's marketing
consulting, which is what we do. We look at our place as a

consultant as it pertains to new product development, emerging technologies, market strategies, and things of that nature.

The first and easiest way to segment the consulting industry is by the functional expertise and by separating out marketing, finance, techs, IT, etc. Then as you go into it, the next reasonable segmentation would be by industry. For example, at McKenzie I believe they have different industry segments for all their groups, as do we. Then the third dimension to this matrix or segmentation strategy would be by the application, and that would be categories such as new product launch, product development, mergers and acquisitions, and so on.

Compensation in Consulting

Your compensation as a consultant depends on the type of application you're working on. For example, suppose you're working on an IT implementation project, and here I believe most companies want a fixed-price contract, rather than an hourly contract. When you go to hourly charges, you're putting a pretty big hole in your boat because things can go way over budget. Someone has to pay for this, either you or your client. A great way to lose a client is to send them a bill they didn't expect.

There are other types of projects where, on the financial side, the clients have a strong preference to pay by what's saved in various processes or systems, and so the payment is a much more risk-based payment. In our sector, on the consulting side, we prefer to work with our clients on an annual subscription base, or what I call a strategic alliance or partnership. We know exactly how much capital we're going to get each month and each year from a client, which allows us to use all of the money we get from the client on their needs. It's actually very unproductive on one level for us if we are continually involved in the bidding process on a project-by-project basis.

There are so many different models of pricing. I think the least effective is the project-by-project model because on the consulting side you have to put the price up to cover the fact that you might not get that agreement, and you also have to include the sales and marketing expenses. For a client, that's not value added or part of the equation.

The Best Characteristics of Consultants

Integrity is the most important trait a consulting firm can have. That's when a company really stands behind its work and behind its people.

You can identify the clients of consulting companies with integrity because they don't end up in legal squabbles with their consulting partners. They don't have long contracts that sign off with penalties and all that. They do most of their work on a handshake or a one-page letter agreement. Those are the ones I respect most, and there aren't many of them. But the ones that run their businesses like that – I am in awe of them.

Managing During Turbulent Times

In my own company it has certainly been a very touchy year, managing through this economic slowdown, because several of my client groups are in what I would call a deep recession and have been for a couple of years. We look very closely at trying to develop a system to match the salary expenses and bonuses we pay to our employees, because at the end of the day, virtually all of the client revenue goes back to the staff. If I can make them know that as we succeed, they succeed, and that the client pays their salaries, not the company, then the focus is on making clients happy, which can generate repeat business. In a slow-down like this, we alter our salary packages to decrease base pay and increase the incentive pay for success, which, of course, is not that motivating in an economic downturn. Everyone understands that this is an economic slow-down, and I think the whole consulting industry is experiencing a certain amount of it right now.

You also have to manage your consulting approach. In turbulent times like these, the customer's viewpoint goes from five years out to the next quarter, so we're working very closely on how to find customer pockets. We want to find the economic forecasts, not for a country's GNP, but for very specific market sectors – medical ultrasounds or specific types of memory chips, for example – so our customers can proactively calibrate their business to what the short-term prospects are going to look like. If we can make our clients proactive to market changes, they're going to save hundreds of millions of dollars. If they continue to produce higher, and the market turns down, and their sales drop off, they've already lost money for two or three months, and they're going to lose money for another two to three months while they restructure. If I can get my consultants to see these changes in advance, they can tell our clients, who can start to proactively recalibrate their business according to where the market's going and save hundreds of millions of dollars.

Managing growth is really important. There are some companies that do well during a recession, and you can do well if you're proactive during a recession. When the economy was booming, every company was going out there very aggressively on acquisition programs. But acquisitions are very expensive in boom times. Now that the economy has slowed down, this is the time companies should be aggressively acquiring new companies. You can get some incredibly good bargains right now on the prices of some companies. What happens instead, though, is that most companies run together like lemmings, and people are not using good strategies right now. Everyone is pulling in their horns instead of taking advantage of the situation. On the merger and acquisitions front, there are great opportunities to increase market share and get rid of key competitors.

Balancing Risk

At Frost and Sullivan, at any given point in time, we like to have 75 percent of our investments in highly risky places in terms of product development and services for our clients and expansion. We do this because my partners and I all derive fun in life and the challenge in business by taking risks and seeing how our ideas work.

Our firm is unique in that our company is owned by a handful of partners, and I don't think any of our partners is motivated by money. We are far more motivated by seeing if our ideas work and how our value-added programs for clients work. So we're always investing that way. I think we take a tremendous amount of risk that I think other more prudent consulting companies wouldn't take. We make some big mistakes, but as the future unrolls, we have very exciting times ahead because we have some very exciting ideas in the pipeline. Every dime we make is reinvested for risky future ideas, so I would say we're probably out of balance on the risky side.

Best Advice

The best piece of advice I've received was from my high school gymnastics coach. He looked at me and said, "Dave, you can't make steak out of hamburger." Probably for the first ten to 15 years of my career, I spent way too much time on either bad projects or people who weren't very well-suited for the consulting industry, and I tried to turn them into first-class consultants. When I thought about what my coach's message was, it caused me to be much, much more aggressive about developing a consulting team that has a similar passion for what we want to do, what we're all committed to, and what we're trying to accomplish. When I see people who don't fit the team, I don't spend time trying to indoctrinate them. I apologize if that sounds a little cold, but I think people who really have a passion for what we're doing make all of our jobs easier.

My best piece of advice regarding balancing life and work was from the person who said, "When a businessman is on his deathbed, he never says he wishes he had spent more time at work." Despite that saying, I think most consultants have a very unhealthy lifestyle, including me. Right now I've been in a hotel for the last 70 days, working on a project. My wife and family aren't exactly thrilled about it.

The best advice is to keep life's bigger picture in front of us all the time, and see our role in it. Remember, God didn't put us on this earth to run a consulting business. I think that gets out of balance for most consultants, as it does for me.

Leadership

Running a consulting company puts profound pressure on developing your leadership skills. In the consulting industry you change projects every day, clients every day, and industries every day. You have a staff of very bright individuals with lots of ideas. They are difficult people to manage because they are so bright, so being a leader in a consulting company is tremendously strenuous and hugely challenging. As I've sat in the leadership post at Frost and Sullivan, what happens over time is that your weaknesses are highlighted more and more as you move forward. It's almost as if you don't gain confidence as a leader, but you learn what great leadership is.

One of those skills is the commitment to and conviction in the direction you're taking your company in. There are so many varied viewpoints and disagreements and arguments about where to take the company, and you don't really have a lot of time to rethink the company's direction every time there's a problem.

To keep an edge in this industry, it is important for the leader to go out and see other CEOs in the client base and other consulting companies. The demands they put on you to keep on top of the game are enormous. The ideas that another CEO can give you in 15 minutes can be worth more than what you'd get in a month or two from your own company. The best way to stay on the edge is to live in the client's company or to take some time out to spend time with other consultants.

Another thing I learned is that you cannot communicate enough. You cannot let communication slow down at any point. People have to know where the company is going, what the major objectives are, and what the status of these objectives is. And you have to give large doses of positive feedback on all of the accomplishments going on in the company.

Staffing a Good Team

I think passion is the underlying component that everyone on a good team has to have. The second thing that greatly increases the client's satisfaction, and even goes well beyond satisfaction, is developing a cross-functional team with multiple disciplines. It goes to that segmentation that I mentioned earlier.

You have several people who have in-depth knowledge of different applications and, in many cases, a cross-cultural team from Asia, Europe, North America, and South America, all with different experience and backgrounds. I think in the past some of the consulting companies were too homogeneous. They were the same race and the same background. I think some of the big consulting companies are starting to see that that doesn't always make it with the client base. Companies we work with are now getting revenues from all over the world. They're facing multi-cultural issues and application issues from all over the world. To increase the probability that you'll find every problem, address every problem, and meet every challenge, you have to have a good team working on it. The projects that are least likely to succeed are managed by one or two people with a similar background, or by two people who get along too well. It's good to have a little friction.

The Golden Rules of Consulting

It sounds very trite but it's very important to be customer-focused, to get inside the client's mind. You have to be able to look at your consulting company through the customer's eyes and not look at the client through your own eyes. It sounds so obvious, but with us, and all our competitors, that has to be the one biggest golden rule.

It's hard to develop this insight because with most consulting companies, as success grows, so does arrogance, and as arrogance grows, so does blindness. That's rule number two: Resist arrogance. I have seen that the attitude that "we know everything, we're on top of everything" in so many consulting companies, even my own. That just doesn't work anymore in the consulting industry. Intimidating the clients with your educational background or knowledge of the industry is just not accepted anymore.

David Frigstad began his career in marketing consulting in 1977, analyzing the trends of high-technology Asian and European direct investment in the United States for the Department of Commerce. In 1980 he began supporting European manufacturers of electronic equipment entering the U.S. market. By 1981 he co-founded Market Intelligence Research Company in Mountain View, California. The company specialized in high-technology marketing consulting, research, and strategy. In 1993 Market Intelligence acquired Frost & Sullivan. The combined company, now called Frost & Sullivan, offers a full line of consulting services, from competitive benchmarking to corporate training, and employs 600 professionals worldwide.

Mr. Frigstad designed the Market Engineering Consulting process from extensive worldwide consulting and business experience. This process creates the foundation and methodology on which Frost & Sullivan performs its consulting and research work. Market Engineering is a measurement-based marketing system designed to drive marketing efficiency and improvement in market position. Mr. Frigstad lectures and trains throughout the world on the Frost & Sullivan Market Engineering System.

Over his career, Mr. Frigstad has authored several books, including Venture Capital Proposal Package, Market Research and Forecasting in the Healthcare Industry, Market Engineering, Competitive Engineering, Customer Engineering, Cost Effective Market Research, High Technology Market Research, and Market Research and Forecasting in Industrial Markets. He is currently working on a new book entitled Strategy Engineering: A Measurement Based Strategy Development System.

Mr. Frigstad has lectured and trained extensively around the world on competitive benchmarking, market engineering, customer engineering, and business strategy. He is a popular speaker at many industry conferences including Competitive Benchmarking in the Telecommunications Industry, the Medical Device Industry Annual Conference, and the Automotive Aftermarket Annual Conference.

Mr. Frigstad holds a Bachelor of Science degree in MIS and management. He received his master's degree in Japanese business administration from the Japan American Institute of Management Science in association with Sophia University, Tokyo, Japan. He also holds a master's degree in business administration with a double concentration in international finance and international marketing from Indiana University.

THE RULES HAVE CHANGED

JOHN C. MCAULIFFE

General Physics Corporation

President

The Excitement of Consulting

The most exciting aspect of consulting is the constant change; clients present new challenges every day. There's constant motion – always new ideas and unique issues. It's a dynamic business, and good consultants are people who embrace new challenges. In fact, much of what we do is related to helping our clients manage the constant change that has become a part of everyday business life. There's a real sense of satisfaction that comes when we provide a solution for a client that can save them money and make them more efficient and more productive.

The advent of learning management systems has created a great deal of excitement in the learning and education arena. Once these systems are implemented, the development of critical business processes and the ability to deliver critical training using technology grow significantly. It also provides the opportunity to outsource large components of the training function, providing the customer with a high level of expertise and significant growth for GP.

Biggest Changes

Advances in technology have been the biggest drivers in consulting. Everybody's trying to do things better and faster; that's going to continue as the pace of technological improvement continues to increase. We've always hired the best and brightest specialists available, and most of our consultants have extensive backgrounds in engineering or specific technical areas, but these days we really place great emphasis on keeping our people ahead of the technology curve. Technology aside, quality consulting will always come down to real human beings working closely together, using their experience to create innovative solutions that benefit the customer; it's really just the tools and the pace that change.

In our history we worked predominantly in regulated industries, so law dictated a lot of the work we did, but today the requirements aren't there. We've had to transform into an organization that provides solutions for companies that need to reduce costs and improve the use of their technology. This has forced us to be more creative and to show a measurable return on the investment for the services we provide. We see a lot of situations now where we may be compensated on an award fee, rather than on a strictly fixed fee. There are a lot of situations these days where metrics are developed to evaluate our performance. That's good for consultants and their customers alike.

The Art of Consulting

An artist sees the world in a unique way, and so do good consultants. Good consultants look at a client situation through the eyes of an expert, rapidly identify issues that are preventing them from reaching their goals, quickly delivering innovative solutions, and then implementing them. Creativity is a big part of it, visualizing the big picture and the details all at once, building a better system in the mind, and then transferring it to the customer via training and technology. True success comes when we conduct the assessment and up-front analysis, and then prove our solution by performing the actual implementation. Delivering only a set of recommendations is akin to a painter producing only sketches; we'd rather deliver a complete, proven piece. Consulting firms that are capable of implementing their own recommendations are going to be successful companies, going forward.

Consultants must also be proficient in the art of relationship building. It's more than just being a "people person." There are specific industry needs out there, and you must be able to communicate effectively with the customer and speak their language. They rely on us for advice, so experience in the industry and a thorough understanding of the customer's concerns are critical to building a trusting relationship.

Understanding Where the Industry is Going

It's important to keep track of the industry, to look outside your own world every now and then. Our staff performs the necessary research to keep us aware of trends occurring both inside and outside our current market sectors, and we also subscribe to research analysts.

The fact is that nobody has a crystal ball; our business can change at any second, based on what happens in the economy and with our customers. That's why we try to stay very close to the client, even if we're not currently on assignment with them. Regular interfaces with the client help us understand where they're going, where they *want* to go, and what issues they're grappling with. It also reminds them that we value our relationship with them. Obviously, being part of trade organizations helps to a certain degree. Internally, we conduct periodic strategic planning meetings to make sure we're heading down the right path and to share knowledge related to the industry and future business prospects.

The Ideal Client Relationship

We know we've become a partner with a client when they've made us part of their strategic plan. That means we've earned their trust, and they respect our judgment. It's always best when we're brought in up front. Coming in late in the game is very difficult because in many cases there will be things that were previously overlooked, and things will have to change, costing the customer more money.

When a client is looking at a learning resource management system, we want to help them do the analysis and the assessment, look at their current processes, and discover what processes need to change once the system is implemented. It's always better to start the relationship with a clean slate and do things right the first time.

Methodologies of Assessment

We follow many of our own branded processes, whether we're assessing a training program, a learning management system, or the ability within an organization to design and develop training. We use a combination of proven processes, along with customized solutions, depending on the situation. It's key to have an assessment process that is rigorous and structured, but also flexible. Each organization is different, and the assessment must not be blind to new situations.

Generally speaking, we take a look at the size of the organization, the type of training that might be needed, the technology that might be available to deliver that training, the reporting and logistics requirements relating to it, and the objectives that the organization wants to reach. We perform assessments that tell them the best way to run that training function. Experience weighs in heavily here, and we've developed a considerable arsenal of best practices based on that experience. We may recommend outsourcing the training, or delivering it in-house. We may have someone administer the program, while we provide a vendor management function, or it may be that we take over the whole training function for the organization. We also determine which business model should be used to best evaluate or measure that training function, whether it should be a cost center or a profit center, and whether it should provide those services internally to the organization or look outside for resources.

Getting up to Speed

At GP, we hire world-class subject matter experts. These people understand specific industries and have extensive experience with the software package or technology that drives their current assignment. That gives us a leg up, but we also count on a fair amount of indoctrination and knowledge transfer from the client and/or the vendor who will be providing the software or technology.

Our people will rapidly get up to speed on the software or technology needed by the company they're working with as part of their assignment, but it's really not enough to just have subject matter expertise in the minds of our people. We're not finished until we've transferred that subject matter expertise to the minds of our clients.

Differences in Firms

There are large consulting firms, for example, Accenture, and then there are niche players – that's where we fit in. Our expertise is on certain market centers of the education arena and the technical area, versus a Price Waterhouse Coopers, which might be a much broader based consulting firm.

Because of the nature of the consulting that we do and the market sectors that we operate in, our ability to bring market expertise is probably the key differentiating factor for us from a place like Accenture. We place heavy emphasis on implementation, not just the pure consulting or assessment components. Larger consulting firms are geared toward the assessment component of the consulting environment.

Turbulent Markets

During a turbulent market or a crisis, it's important to stay focused on clients and the core market sectors. We've tried to grab market share in those arenas, versus trying to branch out significantly. You don't want to be a mile wide and an inch deep in a tough market place. It's best to be operating in a number of core market sectors with core clients for whom we've done a good job and with whom we are able to grow our presence. We've had to make sure that our workforce is somewhat variable. By keeping some full-time employees, some part-time, and some consultants, we can go with the ebbs and flows that come with a turbulent market.

When dealing with our clients, we strive to reduce their costs and increase efficiency and quality. When our clients are focused on slashing their costs, we have to stay focused on helping make their technology and people more efficient and more effective, allowing them to drive waste out of their organization.

It's not easy to profit during a turbulent economy, but one of the things that have helped us is our ability to provide outsourced services. Companies are trying to make their workforce much more variable, so that they can move their cost base with their revenue swings. Outsourcing is a way of doing that.

We have really focused on consulting and the learning resource management area. Learning resource management is a different way of saying outsourcing. Learning resource management systems are enterprise-wide software systems that help large organizations put their hands around the whole training function. It helps with the logistics, the scheduling, the record-keeping, and the development and delivery of the training to the organization. Companies that outsource non-core activities also have more access to expertise. Training is a core competency for us, and our customers get a training initiative that is run like a business by experts in that field. The customers are able to free themselves from the burden of fixed costs, and they receive a top-notch training initiative at the same time.

Risk

Risk is ingrained in the business; there's no way to avoid it. You have to take chances when choosing the customers you want to focus on and the market sectors and services you want to focus on.

As a consulting organization, you have to be constantly providing new and different services. We've tried to keep aware of the market sector, the client base, and the service needs that they're going to be looking for in the future. This will allow us to allocate our dollars to the right places, whether it is the development of new services, hiring new people, or advertising and marketing all of these things.

There are many decisions, many possibilities, but there are no guarantees. Over the last couple of years, we've tried to gather much more information when making decisions than we had in the past. When things are going well, we didn't just wing it, but we might not have done as much research or gained as much knowledge before making decisions as we do today. You don't want to take a risk with only a 50 percent chance of success. In good times, you could do those things, but in tough times, bad decisions are magnified.

Leadership

Intelligence is important for leaders. You have to get the right information and make prudent decisions. Leaders have to have confidence when taking risks. You have to be willing to make tough decisions. Many leaders get into what's called "information gridlock," or they get into a situation where they have to make a tough decision and just can't bring themselves to make it. Leaders need the fortitude to make those decisions regularly.

Sometimes, even after gathering input from your associates and allowing people to have a voice in the process, your decision deviates from their recommendations. Honesty, openness, and communication are critical at this point. You have to explain to them why you're going to take the direction that you're going to take. It's tough to do, but a well-reasoned explanation goes a long way toward getting people on-board.

The leadership model that GP tries to follow is that of "servant leadership," by which leaders are expected to do everything they can to ensure the success of their organization. This model was prompted by a corporate climate survey, conducted to determine the effectiveness of existing leadership and teamwork practices. We actually turned the focus on ourselves this time, subjecting *our own* company to a very tough assessment. The climate survey (needs assessment) identified specific shortcomings in leadership behaviors. A "Leadership Boot Camp" was designed, developed, and rolled out immediately to address leadership training and development and teamwork. The battle-cry of the boot camp is, "Leadership and teamwork drive our performance." Once the top three tiers of corporate leadership were trained, a second climate survey was administered; the results indicated dramatic positive change. What occurred was a dramatic and lasting culture change. GP now has a values-based, employee-driven environment in which every employee is welcomed as a business partner and a fellow steward, responsible and accountable for the company's success.

Sometimes leadership means taking a risk on someone, backing up an employee's new idea, or giving people the freedom to do their job in the way that suits them best. Great leaders earn the respect of their employees and provide an environment that fosters every individual's growth. Leaders must understand people and treat them right. If you do that, people will be willing to come under your leadership and support you when you need it. In the consulting business, if you don't treat people right, you're not in business – you're really nothing without your employees.

Building a Team

We've instituted a behavioral interviewing process within GP. We try to make sure that the people we hire fully understand the job they're going to have. We're looking for people who are willing to travel. That's an unfortunate part of our existence, but it's something people have to understand. We need people who are willing to take on new and different challenges, so we've worked hard to make sure people understand what will be expected of them. Overall, we're looking for people with specific industry expertise and people with strong communications skills.

New employees are trained to understand our dedication to customer service. Consistent with our corporate values, our core internal training course, "Exceptional Customer Service" stresses the importance of carefully managing the relationship and managing every transaction with each of our customers, internal and external. We believe the best way in which to foster "teamwork" is to understand that everyone we deal with is a customer – "our number one customer."

We also do a lot of training in the areas of negotiation, internal performance management, and conflict resolution. We hope all those things combined have given people the tools necessary to handle difficult situations. First and foremost, though, we tell everybody that the best way to deal with conflict is to address it directly. It's important to make sure issues aren't hidden or pushed to the side and to make sure we engage in honest and open communication both with our customers and internally.

It's critical to make sure individuals working on a team bring different strengths to the project, giving the customer access to personnel with diverse proficiencies and knowledge. Some people may be more technically oriented; others may be more business process oriented; and others may be more relationship oriented. What we like to be able to do is to make sure the team covers those bases completely. That's not always easy. Many times we'll be dealing with a lot of individuals who have different agendas or different ideas of what the assignment is really about. It's important to have people that mesh well with the client organization's culture, as well.

Goals and Plans

We have a unique process in our organization for goals and planning. We have a three-year plan that we update annually. It looks at not only next year, but also the year after, and the year after that. A few years ago, we went through an alignment process where we took all the leadership in the organization and refined our vision statement. We aligned ourselves as a unified force in the direction we agreed on, and then arranged the pieces of the organization to fit into that vision.

We then established a set of corporate values based on the alignment process. Most importantly, we participate in the leadership boot camps twice a year. This intensive training instills the leadership in our company with the corporate values and ensures that everyone is aware of the strategic goals of the company. The boot camp format allows for input from everyone for inclusion into the continual strategic planning of the company.

The Future of Consulting

The use of technology is going to expand in our arena, and the ability to deliver training over the Web will be key. Implementing and maintaining these learning management systems is going to be a growth area for the industry as a whole.

I think the whole idea of implementing solutions for non-core competencies is going to be important. You read in the paper every day that 20,000 people are laid off at United Airlines, and 20,000 at American Airlines. These companies want to have a much more variable cost base to better manage the down times; outsourcing is the key. After ten great years of virtual growth, companies got out of the habit of being cost-conscious and having business models that allow for ups and downs. This will teach us a lesson that in industry we have to have a more variable cost base.

The Golden Rules of Consulting

Know your customer; subject matter expertise is key. Consultants must understand the details about the client's business, their issues, their industry, and their technology.

Consultants must be excellent communicators. You may have the best answers in the world, but if you can't articulate them, they're worthless.

Solutions that consultants bring to clients must have tangible results. There must be a measurable return on investment, whether it's increased productivity, reduced cost, new technology, or getting more out of the current technology. Our customers spend a lot of money on our services; they deserve an excellent return on that investment.

Stick to your values in good times and in bad times. It's really easy in tough times to abandon the things that have made you successful. In bad times you have to remember what made you successful as a company and as an individual. You have to keep in mind that tough times are generally brief. Companies that stick to their values come out all right.

People who get into roles of leadership get there because they're generally pretty intelligent, but also because they're willing to work very hard. Working hard means working smart. There has to be a balance in your life, and there are times when it has to be time to go home. You can't feel guilty because you didn't work a 14-hour day. Some days it's okay to work less. No matter who you are, your life needs to be balanced. In the long term, you'll be a better person and a better employee. If your life isn't balanced, problems are going to creep into your work life and have a major impact.

Read. Everyone in this industry has to do a lot of reading to keep up with things.

Work hard to be in touch with customers on a consistent basis, so they know you're there; you're hearing their problems; and you're hearing their issues. Internally, it's important to stay in touch with people and have constant discussions within the organization.

As president of General Physics (GP), John C. McAuliffe has guided the strategy and operations that have made GP a world leader in performance improvement services. GP provides consulting, training, and technical and engineering services to Fortune 1000 companies.

Before being named president, Mr. McAuliffe served as the company's chief operating officer and chief financial officer. In addition, he is a member of the board of directors of GP's corporate parent, GP Strategies Corporation. Before joining General Physics, Mr. McAuliffe worked for Arthur Andersen after graduating from Loyola College in Baltimore, Maryland.

ASPATORE BUSINESS REVIEW
Tear Out This Page and Mail or Fax To:

**Aspatore Books, PO Box 883, Bedford, MA 01730
Or Fax To (617) 249-1970**

Name:

Email:

Shipping Address:

City: State: Zip:

Billing Address:

City: State: Zip:

Phone:

Lock in at the Current Rates Today-Rates Increase Every Year
Please Check the Desired Length Subscription:

1 Year ($1,090) _____   2 Years (Save 10%-$1,962) _____
5 Years (Save 20%-$4,360) _____   10 Years (Save 30%-$7,630) _____
Lifetime Subscription ($24,980) _____

(If mailing in a check you can skip this section but please read fine print below and sign below)
Credit Card Type (Visa & Mastercard & Amex):

Credit Card Number:

Expiration Date:

Signature:

Would you like us to automatically bill your credit card at the end of your
subscription so there is no discontinuity in service? (You can still cancel your
subscription at any point before the renewal date.) Please circle: Yes   No

***(Please note the billing address much match the address on file with your credit
card company exactly)**

Terms & Conditions
We shall send a confirmation receipt to your email address. If ordering from Massachusetts, please add
5% sales tax on the order (not including shipping and handling). If ordering from outside of the US, an
additional $51.95 per year will be charged for shipping and handling costs. All issues are paperback and
will be shipped as soon as they become available. Sorry, no returns or refunds at any point unless
automatic billing is selected, at which point you may cancel at any time before your subscription is
renewed (no funds shall be returned however for the period currently subscribed to). Issues that are not
already published will be shipped upon publication date. Publication dates are subject to delay-please
allow 1-2 weeks for delivery of first issue. If a new issue is not coming out for another month, the issue
from the previous quarter will ·be sent for the first issue. For the most up to date information on
publication dates and availability please visit www.Aspatore.com.

Inside the Minds: Leading CEOs (ISBN: 1587620553)

Industry Leaders Share Their Knowledge on Management, Motivating Others, and Profiting in Any Economy - *Inside the Minds: Leading CEOs* features some of the biggest name, proven CEOs in the world. These highly acclaimed CEOs share their knowledge on management, the Internet and technology, client relationships, compensation, motivating others, building and sustaining a profitable business in any economy and making a difference at any level within an organization.

Inside the Minds: Internet Bigwigs (ISBN: 1587620103)

Industry Experts Forecast the Future of the Internet Economy (After the Shakedown) - *Inside the Minds: Internet Bigwigs* features a handful of the leading minds of the Internet and technology revolution. These individuals include executives from Excite (Founder), Beenz.com (CEO), Organic (CEO), Agency.com (Founder), Egghead (CEO), Credite Suisse First Boston (Internet Analyst), CIBC (Internet Analyst) and Sandbox.com. Items discussed include killer-apps for the 21st century, the stock market, emerging industries, international opportunities, and a plethora of other issues affecting anyone with a "vested interest" in the Internet and technology revolution.

Bigwig Briefs: Management & Leadership (ISBN: 1587620146)

Industry Experts Reveal the Secrets How to Get There, Stay There, and Empower Others That Work For You

Bigwig Briefs: Management & Leadership includes knowledge excerpts from some of the leading executives in the business world. These highly acclaimed executives explain how to break into higher ranks of management, how to become invaluable to your company, and how to empower your team to perform to their utmost potential.

Bigwig Briefs: The Golden Rules of the Internet Economy (After the Shakedown) (ISBN: 1587620138)

Industry Experts Reveal the Most Important Concepts From the First Phase of the Internet Economy

Bigwig Briefs: The Golden Rules of the Internet Economy includes knowledge excerpts from some of the leading business executives in the Internet and Technology industries. These highly acclaimed executives explain where the future of the Internet economy is heading, mistakes to avoid for companies of all sizes, and the keys to long term success.

Bigwig Briefs: Start-ups Keys to Success (ISBN: 1587620170)

Industry Experts Reveal the Secrets to Launching a Successful New Venture

Bigwig Briefs: Start-ups Keys to Success includes knowledge excerpts from some of the leading VCs, CEOs CFOs, CTOs and business executives in every industry. These highly acclaimed executives explain the secrets behind the financial, marketing, business development, legal, and technical aspects of starting a new venture.

Bigwig Briefs: Become a VP of Marketing (ISBN 1587620707)

Leading Marketing VPs Reveal What it Takes to Get There, Stay There, and Empower Others That Work With You - *Bigwig Briefs: Become a VP of Marketing* includes knowledge excerpts from VPs of Marketing from companies such as Ford, Home Depot, GE, Coke and more. These highly acclaimed VPs of Marketing explain the secrets behind keeping your marketing skills sharp, working with a team, empowering positive change within an organization, working with your boss, utilizing your "special" marketing talents, getting noticed, motivating others and other important topics.

Inside the Minds: Leading Advertisers (ISBN: 1587620545)
Industry Leaders Share Their Knowledge on the Future of Building Brands Through Advertising – *Inside the Minds: Leading Advertisers* features CEOs/Presidents from agencies such as Young & Rubicam, Leo Burnett, Ogilvy, Saatchi & Saatchi, Interpublic Group, Valassis, Grey Global Group and FCB Worldwide. These leading advertisers share their knowledge on the future of the advertising industry, the everlasting effects of the Internet and technology, client relationships, compensation, building and sustaining brands, and other important topics.

Inside the Minds: Internet Marketing (ISBN: 1587620022)
Industry Experts Reveal the Secrets to Marketing, Advertising, and Building a Successful Brand on the Internet - *Inside the Minds: Internet Marketing* features leading marketing VPs from some of the top Internet companies in the world including Buy.com, 24/7 Media, DoubleClick, Guerrilla Marketing, Viant, MicroStrategy, MyPoints.com, WineShopper.com, Advertising.com and eWanted.com. Their experiences, advice, and stories provide an unprecedented look at the various online and offline strategies involved with building a successful brand on the Internet for companies in every industry. Also examined is calculating return on investment, taking an offline brand online, taking an online brand offline, where the future of Internet marketing is heading, and numerous other issues.

Bigwig Briefs: Guerrilla Marketing (ISBN 1587620677)
The Best of Guerrilla Marketing
Best selling author Jay Levinson shares the now world famous principles behind guerrilla marketing, in the first ever "brief" written on the subject. Items discussed include the Principles Behind Guerrilla Marketing, What Makes a Guerrilla, Attacking the Market, Everyone Is a Marketer, Media Matters, Technology and the Guerrilla Marketer, and Dollars and Sense. A must have for any big time marketing executive, small business owner, entrepreneur, marketer, advertiser, or any one interested in the amazing, proven power of guerrilla marketing.

Bigwig Briefs: The Art of Deal Making (ISBN: 1587621002)
Leading Deal Makers Reveal the Secrets to Negotiating, Leveraging Your Position and Inking Deals - *Bigwig Briefs: The Art of Deal Making* includes knowledge excerpts from some of the biggest name CEOs, Lawyers, VPs of BizDev and Investment Bankers in the world on ways to master the art of deal making. These highly acclaimed deal makers from companies such as Prudential, Credite Suisse First Boston, Barclays, Hogan & Hartson, Proskaur Rose, AT&T and others explain the secrets behind keeping your deal skills sharp, negotiations, working with your team, meetings schedules and environment, deal parameters and other important topics. A must have for every financial professional, lawyer, business development professional, CEO, entrepreneur and individual involved in deal making in any environment and at every level.

Other Best Selling Business Books Include:

Inside the Minds: Leading Accountants
Inside the Minds: Leading CTOs
Inside the Minds: Leading Deal Makers
Inside the Minds: Leading Wall St. Investors
Inside the Minds: Leading Investment Bankers
Inside the Minds: Internet BizDev
Inside the Minds: Internet CFOs
Inside the Minds: Internet Lawyers
Inside the Minds: The New Health Care Industry
Inside the Minds: The Financial Services Industry
Inside the Minds: The Media Industry
Inside the Minds: The Real Estate Industry
Inside the Minds: The Automotive Industry
Inside the Minds: The Telecommunications Industry
Inside the Minds: The Semiconductor Industry
Bigwig Briefs: Term Sheets & Valuations
Bigwig Briefs: Venture Capital
Bigwig Briefs: Become a CEO
Bigwig Briefs: Become a CTO
Bigwig Briefs: Become a VP of BizDev
Bigwig Briefs: Become a CFO
Bigwig Briefs: Small Business Internet Advisor
Bigwig Briefs: Human Resources & Building a Winning Team
Bigwig Briefs: Career Options for Law School Students
Bigwig Briefs: Career Options for MBAs
Bigwig Briefs: Online Advertising
OneHourWiz: Becoming a Techie
OneHourWiz: Stock Options
OneHourWiz: Public Speaking
OneHourWiz: Making Your First Million
OneHourWiz: Internet Freelancing
OneHourWiz: Personal PR & Making a Name For Yourself
OneHourWiz: Landing Your First Job
OneHourWiz: Internet & Technology Careers (After the Shakedown)

Go to www.Aspatore.com for a
Complete List of Titles!

**ASPATORE
BOOKS**